175 best babycakes® cupcake maker recipes

Easy recipes for bite-size cupcakes, cheesecakes, mini pies and more!

Kathy Moore & Roxanne Wyss

Robert ROSE

175 Best Babycakes Cupcake Maker Recipes

For complete cataloguing information, see page 209.

Disclaimer
The recipes in this book have been carefully tested by our kitchen and our tasters. To the best of our knowledge, they are safe and nutritious for ordinary use and users. For those people with food or other allergies, or who have special food requirements or health issues, please read the suggested contents of each recipe carefully and determine whether or not they may create a problem for you. All recipes are used at the risk of the consumer. Consumers should always consult the Babycakes manual for recommended procedures and cooking times.

We cannot be responsible for any hazards, loss or damage that may occur as a result of any recipe use.

For those with special needs, allergies, requirements or health problems, in the event of any doubt, please contact your medical adviser prior to the use of any recipe.

Design and Production: Daniella Zanchetta/PageWave Graphics Inc.
Editor: Sue Sumeraj
Recipe editor: Jennifer MacKenzie
Copy editor: Kelly Jones
Proofreader: Sheila Wawanash
Indexer: Gillian Watts
Photographer: Colin Erricson
Associate Photographer: Matt Johannsson
Food Stylist: Kathryn Robertson
Prop Stylist: Charlene Erricson

Cover image: Princess Pink Party Cupcakes (page 37)

We acknowledge the financial support of the Government of Canada through the Book Publishing Industry Development Program (BPIDP) for our publishing activities.

Published by Robert Rose Inc.
120 Eglinton Avenue East, Suite 800, Toronto, Ontario, Canada M4P 1E2
Tel: (416) 322-6552 Fax: (416) 322-6936
www.robertrose.ca

Printed and bound in Canada

2 3 4 5 6 7 8 9 TCP 19 18 17 16 15 14 13 12 11

Contents

Acknowledgments

IT TAKES A very supportive community to complete a cookbook, and we are very grateful to the many people who have assisted, inspired and encouraged us and this book in so many ways.

Each of us is very thankful for our families, and it is love for our families that centers us and allows us to share our passion for food with you. There are no words to express our gratitude for all of the taste testing they did, the understanding and encouragement they gave us and the dishes they washed as this cookbook was written.

Kathy's family — David, Laura and Amanda — circle her in love and joy and are the inspiration and support for every dream. Thanks to them, every Moore family dinner is special and memorable.

Roxanne's family — Bob and Grace — add sweetness and love to her life every day, and she thanks them for their endless support and patience during intense work projects and for always enthusiastically accompanying her on her foodie field trips when they travel. She would also like to thank her mom and dad, Colleen and Kenny Wyss, who taught her that great food, Sunday dinners and family make life complete.

Special thanks to Bob Dees of Robert Rose for believing in us and this book, and to all of the talented people at Robert Rose who cared, challenged us and contributed to making this book the best it could be. We so appreciate Sue Sumeraj, our editor, for her extraordinary expertise and insight and are grateful to Jennifer MacKenzie, our recipe editor, for sharing her extensive food knowledge and skill with us. In a cookbook, the design and photographs make the recipes come alive. We appreciate the talent of Daniella Zanchetta of PageWave Graphics, who created the beautiful design.

For the stunning photographs, we wish to thank the team of Colin Erricson, Matt Johannsson, Kathryn Robertson and Charlene Erricson. Thanks also to copy editor Kelly Jones, proofreader Sheila Wawanash and indexer Gillian Watts for their careful attention to detail. What a talented, dedicated team they all are.

We want to thank our agents, Sally Ekus, Lisa Ekus and the entire staff at The Lisa Ekus Group, LLC, for unparalleled insight and support.

This book really began thanks to our friendship with Select Brands, and we are grateful for being part of their team. Bill Endres, Debby Endres, Eric Endres, Wesley Endres, Karen Hong, Mark Krasne, Tim Lambert, Patty Lehn, Scott Royal-Ferris, Laura Tornini, Blaise Wooderson and the entire group make this company very special. Truly each and every person at the company has our thanks for their work and for their commitment to making the Babycakes cupcake maker a reality. You are all shining stars!

We sometimes need colleagues to nudge us on and — more importantly — to believe in us, and that is so true of this book. Special thanks to Judith Fertig and Karen Adler, cookbook authors and friends, for opening doors, paving pathways and inspiring us on the journey.

Recipe development always takes inspiration, followed by tests and retests. So many foodie friends inspire us daily. Among them is Jill Silva, Food Editor of the James Beard Award–winning food section of the *Kansas City Star*, who trusts us to regularly develop recipes for the "Eating for Life" column. The members of Roxanne's monthly cookbook club have been a wonderful source of friendship and support. These longtime foodie friends include Karen Adler, Dee Barwick, Liz Benson, Judith Fertig, Vicki Johnson, Gayle Parnow and Kathy Smith.

We are blessed because so many incredible people support us and our work, and while space may limit us from thanking each of you by name, please know that we appreciate you all. We are so grateful to our families, friends and neighbors for taste-testing and critiquing. Two of special note, Jessica Swiecicki and Julie Bondank, were essential as we tested and retested recipes, and we know we couldn't have met our deadline without you.

It's hard to believe 30 years have passed since we began working together in a corporate test kitchen. It is so special that we are still working together, dreaming together and stretching our boundaries together. The laughter, support, caring and trust we share inspires and sustains our work.

About the Electrified Cooks™

WE ARE Kathy Moore and Roxanne Wyss, and we are the Electrified Cooks. We both studied food in college, and we come from a test kitchen background and are home economists. We first worked together in the test kitchen of a small appliance company soon after college. We tested appliances, wrote recipes and answered consumers' questions for years — and we loved it.

We loved it so much that we joined forces and have worked together ever since. We have been consulting with food and appliance companies for many years, bringing our test kitchen skills, our knowledge of food trends and our real-world food experiences to all that we do. Whether it is teaching classes, developing recipes or blogging (www.pluggedintocooking.com), we love everything about cooking, and we want to share the most relevant, factual information with you. We want to empower you to be able to go home and cook something wonderful. We want to provide you with the best tips and how-to information so that cooking is easy and successful for you.

Our focus has always been on the home cook and answering the everyday challenge of "What's for supper?" This, plus our specialization in small appliances, led us to Select Brands. We have worked with the president and owner of Select Brands, William Endres, for many, many years. The Select Brands team is a special one, and we are fortunate to work with them. When the Babycakes concept came to us for initial testing and recipe development, it was a natural fit. The fact that we keep using the Babycakes cupcake maker and still love to serve the freshly made cupcakes, pies and appetizers we bake in it is a testament to its value.

We really are very close friends. We love working together and sharing the joy and laughter of the journey. At the same time, we have different tastes. So, when we say that one of us enjoys vanilla and the other chocolate, it's true.

5

Introduction

WE ARE KNOWN for our energy, laughter and the overall excitement we bring with us to every project. We love to cook, and we use appliances all the time. Our passion and our pastime is cooking, so when we say that one new appliance stands head and shoulders above the rest, you can take our word for it.

We adore the Babycakes cupcake maker. It is nonstop fun, and it cooks wonderfully. We fell in love with the concept the very first minute we heard about it one day at the Select Brands office. We were thrilled when we saw the first prototype, and we are still crazy about it even after developing all the recipes for this book.

So what can the Babycakes cupcake maker do? It not only makes yummy cupcakes and hand pies, it can also be used to cook other desserts and even appetizers! We have often heard it described as an Easy-Bake Oven for adults.

Miniature cupcakes follow on the heels of the popular cupcake trend, but because they are bite-size, they are even more appealing because they provide all the flavor of a scrumptious sweet without the same level of guilt.

Babycakes are perfect for all ages. Adults savor them at office and cocktail parties, and children (from princesses to pirates, toddlers to teens) enjoy them at school events, scout parties and gatherings big and small.

The introduction of Babycakes by Select Brands created a new, exciting product category in the housewares industry. Sure, there are other appliances out there that can bake cupcakes and small pies, but Babycakes was the first, and we think it's the best on offer. There are lots of Babycakes features to love. We like the size of the cupcake wells and the pie crimp on each well; the pie cutter tools make welcome additions to your kitchen, too. You'll discover that the recipes for cupcakes, hand pies, appetizers and other goodies in this book will produce tiny, two-bite treats, but they are pure fun and they taste great. It's true: the best things come in small packages.

How to Use the Babycakes Cupcake Maker

YOU WILL FIND the Babycakes cupcake maker so easy to use. Reading these few simple steps and tips will enable you to have the most fun with the least amount of effort.

Preheating

It is not necessary to preheat the Babycakes cupcake maker when baking cupcakes and muffins — though, once it is hot, you can make batch after batch. And don't preheat when making hand pies, tarts, shells and cups — we don't want you to burn your fingers!

Paper Liners and Nonstick Spray

Paper liners make Babycakes easy to bake and serve — and they make the Babycakes cupcake maker easier to clean, too. For cupcakes and muffins, they are a convenience but are not required. Paper liners are a must, though, for cheesecakes, brownie bites and a few other foods. Without paper liners, these items are nearly impossible to remove from the wells without burning your fingers, and even if you manage to get them out, using a tool of some kind, the soft, hot batter is liable to ooze. Paper liners are not used for hand pies, pie crusts for tarts, phyllo cups or tortilla cups. The recipes in this book specify when paper liners are required or are optional.

The ideal paper liners to use are ones that are sized specifically for the Babycakes cupcake wells, available through Select Brands (www.selectbrands. com or www.thebabycakesshop.com). We have also used specialty paper liners purchased from cake decorating supply shops and candy shops, and these work well too. Try paper liners that measure $1\frac{5}{8}$ inches (4 cm) in diameter, sometimes labeled "candy papers" (for example, for chocolate peanut butter cups). Just make sure the liner is not taller than the cupcake wells.

If you are not using paper liners, nonstick spray may be used instead. Just spray the wells before spooning in the batter, and spray again as necessary between batches if you begin to see a bit of sticking.

Mixing the Batter

While we both own large, heavy-duty mixers, we used a hand mixer to test all of the recipes in this book. You only need a small amount of batter to make Babycakes, so you really don't need to use a large mixer. Because speed, power and beater design vary from mixer to mixer, the speeds listed in the recipes are guidelines only; you may need to adjust the speed on your mixer to get the best results.

Filling the Wells

The easiest way to fill the wells is with a small scoop. The ideal scoop, sometimes called a disher, holds about 1 tablespoon (15 mL) and has a spring-action "scraper" to push the batter out of the scoop. Small scoops, often sold for dipping cookie dough, can be purchased at kitchen and specialty shops. If you don't have a small scoop, you can use a small measuring cup to ladle the batter into the Babycakes wells.

For cupcakes and muffins, fill the wells until they are almost full — about three-quarters full, or even a little more. (Of course, don't overfill them, as the batter might spread to the surface area surrounding the wells.) An average Babycakes cupcake or muffin would use about 1½ tablespoons (22 mL) of batter, but you might use as little as 1 tablespoon (15 mL) or as much as 2 tablespoons (30 mL). Factors such as viscosity of batter and whether you are using a paper liner (and, if so, what kind of liner) can also affect how much you should fill the wells. After you use the Babycakes cupcake maker a few times, you may develop a preference for larger or smaller cupcakes and muffins. We find that some of our friends like slightly larger cupcakes and muffins, and others slightly smaller. Both are okay. Make them your own way. No matter which size you choose, we recommend that you are consistent in the batch — no one wants a tiny cupcake or muffin next to a larger one on the same serving plate, and you want them to bake in the same amount of time.

The number of cupcakes or muffins you get from a recipe will be affected by how much batter you use for each. When measurements are so small, adding just an extra teaspoon (5 mL) of batter to a few cupcakes or muffins can make a big difference to the final tally and could reduce the number of cupcakes or muffins you get from a recipe by three or four — or more. The volume listed in each recipe is an estimate based on our tests and an average-size cupcake or muffin.

Filling only some of the wells is okay. In our testing, we occasionally found a slight variation in baking time or slightly uneven baking — but we had to put on our critical test kitchen hats and glasses to see it. If the last bit of the batter only makes three or four cupcakes or muffins, that is fine. Bake them anyway — they are too good to waste.

Baking

Once the wells are filled, shut the top of the Babycakes cupcake maker. You should hear it click. Set a timer and check the baking progress after about 5 minutes. Most cupcakes and muffins bake for about 5 to 8 minutes. The cupcakes and muffins are done cooking when a tester inserted in the center comes out clean. Hint: We often check the doneness of *each* cupcake or muffin — even slight variations (such as the amount of batter in the wells, or the order in which you filled the wells) will affect the baking time. It is best to check several.

Babycakes bake quickly, so be careful not to overcook them, as they will become dry.

Removing Babycakes from the Wells

A fork tool from Select Brands is perfectly designed to help lift the delicate hot cupcakes and muffins out of the wells and can be ordered from the Babycakes website (www.thebabycakesshop.com). Alternatively, you can use a small offset spatula, with a blade of about $4\frac{1}{2}$ inches (11 cm). The blade is small and thin enough to easily lift the edge of cupcakes, muffins, hand pies, tarts and cheesecakes. Be very careful not to scrape the coating on the Babycakes cupcake maker. (You'll notice that the appliance's instructions caution against using metals on the nonstick coating.)

Set the baked cupcakes, muffins, pies or other items on a wire rack to cool. Then, if you have more batter, bake another batch. We do lots of successive batches right in a row, especially when we are at shows and events. Just keep 'em going! The exception: if you are baking pies or cups that need pressing down into the wells, unplug the unit and let it cool for a few minutes so you don't burn your fingers.

Making Cupcakes

You can bake 8 miniature cupcakes at a time, each about two bites. You can bake just one batch in about 6 to 8 minutes — or bake batch after batch.

You can bake just about any cake recipe or cake mix in the Babycakes cupcake maker. In this book, you will find both from-scratch recipes and recipes that begin with a cake mix — and both work equally well. One exception: angel food cake mixes and sponge-type cakes are best baked in a conventional oven and not in Babycakes. We also find that different brands of cake mix bake a little differently and have a different taste. Experiment to see which brand you prefer.

Prepare the batter for from-scratch Babycakes cupcakes the same way you would prepare batter to be cooked in an oven. First, combine the dry ingredients. In another bowl, beat the sugar and fat until creamy, then beat in the eggs. Beat in the dry ingredients alternately with the recipe's liquid (such as buttermilk), making three additions of dry and two of wet.

Smaller recipes, like the ones we have developed for this book, may be preferable, as some batters yield a lot more cupcakes than you might want at one time. If you have a tried-and-true family favorite cake recipe, we bet it will also make wonderful miniature two-bite cupcakes, but you may want to cut the recipe in half.

If you use a cake mix instead of a from-scratch recipe, you'll find that half of a standard two-layer cake mix makes about 28 to 30 Babycakes. Use this standard recipe as a guide:

2 cups	cake mix	500 mL
2	eggs, at room temperature	2
10 tbsp	water	150 mL
$\frac{1}{4}$ cup	vegetable oil	60 mL

1. In a medium bowl, using an electric mixer on low speed, beat cake mix, eggs, water and oil for 30 seconds or until moistened. Beat on medium speed for 2 minutes.

Storing Cupcakes

If you are not frosting your cupcakes within an hour after cooling them, be sure to cover them or pack them in an airtight container to prevent them from drying out.

Most cupcakes can be stored and sealed in an airtight container at room temperature for up to 3 days. Those that are topped with cream cheese frosting or whipped cream must be stored in the refrigerator.

Cupcakes freeze well. Bake them and let them cool to room temperature on wire racks, then seal them in an airtight container, separating the layers with parchment or waxed paper. Typical sealable food storage bags are not really airtight; instead, use freezer bags or plastic food storage containers. If properly sealed, cupcakes can be stored in the freezer for up to 3 months. Let cupcakes thaw at room temperature for about an hour before serving.

Cupcakes freeze best if not frosted. It's better to frost when you are ready to serve them.

Storing Cheesecakes

Cheesecakes must be kept in the refrigerator. Since they contain eggs, they should be served chilled. Even for a buffet or party, keep them refrigerated and serve just what will be eaten soon. They should not sit at room temperature for longer than 2 hours.

Cheesecakes freeze beautifully. Refrigerate freshly baked cheesecakes until they're well chilled, then seal them in an airtight container or freezer bag, separating the layers with parchment or waxed paper, and freeze for up to 2 months. Let them thaw overnight in the refrigerator before serving.

Storing Other Treats

Muffins can be stored in the freezer for up to 3 months. Double-crust fruit-filled and meat-filled hand pies can be frozen for up to 2 months. Do not freeze cream-filled pies, such as coconut cream pie. In all cases, make sure to let the baked goods cool completely first, then seal them in an airtight container or freezer bag, separating the layers with parchment or waxed paper.

How to Clean the Babycakes Cupcake Maker

Generally, cleanup is simple. Just unplug the Babycakes cupcake maker and let it cool completely. Wipe the surfaces with a damp cloth. Use a dry paper towel to absorb any residual oils.

There may be times when a damp cloth can't get the appliance clean. For those rare instances, first unplug the appliance, then, while the unit is still warm, wet a kitchen towel or paper towel and place it across the inner surface of the appliance. Close the unit and let it steam for about 5 minutes or until the towel is just cool enough to touch. The sugars and any other residuals will wipe off easily. Always use caution, and never place the towel in the appliance if it is plugged in.

The plates of the appliance do not come out, and there is nothing to take apart. Do not use soap or abrasive cleaners on it.

The Babycakes Pantry

WHAT IS IN a well-stocked Babycakes pantry? Keeping a few basic supplies handy — cake mixes, flour, dried buttermilk, sugar and butter — will make baking more convenient. Watch for sales, so you can stock up; fall and the weeks leading up to Christmas are common times for sales on these items. (We stock up on butter and keep it frozen until needed.) Generic store brands are often just as good as the top-label products; experiment to find out which brands work best.

Although baking in the Babycakes cupcake maker is almost foolproof, why not try to get the very best flavor out of each and every morsel you bake? In this section you'll find our best tips on the ingredients we recommend and use.

Always remember to measure carefully. This is not the time to guess, or to cook by looks and handfuls. Baking requires accurate measuring.

Flour

We use all-purpose flour in these recipes. For the most part, it is not necessary to purchase bread flour, pastry flour, cake flour, whole wheat flour or any other specialty flour. Gluten-free recipes, however, require gluten-free flour, and this is specified in those recipes.

The best flours for baking are those that have a high enough protein level to create structure and yet are tender enough for pastry and muffins. While the differences in various all-purpose flours are subtle, we like King Arthur unbleached all-purpose flour for baking. We also really like Hudson Cream flour, a great artisanal flour made by the Stafford County Flour Mills Company, an independent mill. (Maybe we are showing our midwestern roots, since Hudson Cream flour is milled in Kansas.) Do you have to buy these flours? No, of course not. But, being foodies, we want to share our sage advice and fun food finds.

It's important to measure flour properly, especially with such small quantities. Spoon the flour from the canister or flour sack into a dry measuring cup and level it off with a knife or straight edge. Do not dip the measuring cup into the flour — it will compact the flour and you will end up with more flour than called for in the recipe. Don't tap the measuring cup or pack it down. There is no need to sift the flour.

Sugar

Granulated sugar adds not only a sweet flavor but also tenderness to baked goods. None of the recipes in this book were tested using artificial sweeteners.

Brown sugar is always measured packed into the measuring cup. You can use either light or dark brown sugar in any of the recipes, but dark brown sugar has a slightly richer flavor. Most people choose the brown sugar they are most familiar with. Given a choice, Roxanne chooses dark brown sugar, while Kathy favors light.

There is no need to sift confectioners' (icing) sugar in these recipes. In fact, we have found that you rarely need to sift confectioners' sugar anymore. It generally blends into the icing smoothly, especially when you are using an electric mixer. If you feel it is necessary to sift the confectioners' sugar, sift it after measuring.

Eggs

All of the recipes in this book use large eggs. Extra-large eggs or smaller eggs will give different results. You'll get the best results if you bring eggs to room temperature before baking with them.

Butter

We use real butter for most recipes, and we use unsalted butter for baking. The recipes were tested with butter, not margarine. Most recipes call for softened butter, which means it should be set out at room temperature for about 30 minutes before baking. If you forget this step, slice the butter into slabs, place it on a microwave-safe glass plate and microwave on Medium-Low (20%) power for 10 to 15 seconds for ¼ cup (60 mL) butter, or 20 to 25 seconds for ½ cup (125 mL) butter, until it just starts to soften. Let butter stand for about 10 minutes, then proceed with the recipe. Do not microwave the butter until it melts unless the recipe specifically states to melt it.

Lower-fat butter and imitation spreads have different moisture and fat contents, and using them may affect the flavor, the texture and the baking. We don't recommend using them for these recipes.

Buttermilk

Many cake recipes begin with buttermilk. Not only does it add a wonderful tang to the flavor, but the acidity in buttermilk plays a special role with the leavening. Cakes and muffins that use buttermilk generally rely on baking soda.

In a pinch and don't have buttermilk? Pour 1 tbsp (15 mL) white vinegar or lemon juice into a 1-cup (250 mL) measure and add enough milk to reach the 1-cup (250 mL) line. Let stand for 5 to 10 minutes, until it thickens, then proceed with the recipe.

Dried buttermilk is also readily available and, when reconstituted according to package instructions, can be used in place of fresh buttermilk. Keep a can handy in the pantry.

Sour Cream and Cream Cheese

The recipes in this book were tested with regular, full-fat dairy products. Lower-fat cream cheese or lower-fat sour cream deliver slightly different flavors, and — more importantly — their formulas may affect the composition of the baked goods. But since Babycakes cupcakes are just a couple of bites, there's no need to feel guilty about using the full-fat ingredients.

Vanilla

Pure vanilla extract is our choice for the best, purest flavor. Imitation vanilla may cost less, but the flavor is not as intense.

Fun with Babycakes

BAKING CUPCAKES IN your Babycakes cupcake maker is only half the fun — you also get to let your creativity shine by frosting and decorating them!

Frosting Cupcakes

Let cupcakes cool before frosting — for at least 30 minutes, if possible. If they're frosted while warm, the frosting will melt.

The Babycakes cupcake maker comes with an icing bag and decorating tips, but you may want to purchase more. Sometimes you'll want to have several different icing bags on the go, filled with different colors of frosting. Or you may have helpers who each need their own bag. Many people prefer to use disposable bags, as there's no risk that they're harboring bacteria. Disposable icing bags are readily available at many craft stores and shops that sell cake decorating supplies. If you don't have enough tips, you can cut the point off the bag and pipe the frosting that way. And if you don't have enough icing bags, no problem! Just fill a sealable food storage bag, seal it and cut the tip off a corner.

Our favorite tips are Wilton #12 and #22. We usually put a nice little dollop, swirl or star on the top center of each cupcake. Even if we use more frosting than that, we like to leave a bit of the cupcake showing around the edges; that edge of cupcake is especially pretty if the color of the cake and the color of the frosting contrast. The amount of frosting you use on each cupcake is totally up to you.

Filling an icing bag is easy. Fold the top of the bag down around itself, like a sleeve cuff, so that 2 to 3 inches (5 to 7.5 cm) is folded over. If you are using a decorating tip, push it through the bag to the tip, or add the coupler so that you can change tips while the bag is still full. Spoon the frosting into the bag, filling it about half full. Roll up the sides and twist the top shut. Use a rubber band to prevent frosting from squirting out the top — especially if kids are helping. Then gently squeeze the icing bag from the top down, pushing the frosting out through the tip.

We developed the frosting recipes in this book so that each would nicely frost a typical batch of cupcakes. For example, 1¾ cups (425 mL) of Buttercream Frosting (page 80) will frost 24 to 32 cupcakes if you pipe on the frosting. If you like to frost cupcakes with a tall swirl of frosting or you prefer to spoon it on a little thicker, the same amount may frost 12 to 16 cupcakes; in that case, you may need to increase the frosting recipe by half or even double it.

The flavor of the cupcake and the frosting should complement one another, but they do not have to match. For example, while chocolate frosting on chocolate cupcakes is a really good combination, who can resist a Red Velvet Cupcake (page 25) topped with Cream Cheese Frosting (page 90)?

If you like, you can tint the frosting to the desired color. Gels and pastes offer intense coloring and come in a wide variety of colors. Cake decorating supply shops sell lots of new products — including edible markers, sprays and other products that enable you to create just the right look.

Leftover frosting can be stored in an airtight container in the refrigerator for up to 2 weeks. Let frosting come to room temperature before using it again.

Alternatives to Frosting

Not every cupcake needs frosting to look beautiful. Try something different, like Lemon Glaze (page 93) or Chocolate Drizzle (page 92). Here are some other pretty alternatives to frosting:

- Dust the cupcakes with confectioners' (icing) sugar, unsweetened cocoa powder or cinnamon-sugar. To get a light, even coating, sift the dusting though a tea strainer. For a fun pattern, try using a stencil over a smooth glaze or a plain cupcake. You can use smaller stencils, one part of a large stencil or a creation of your own.
- Serve cupcakes topped with fresh berries and a drizzle of strawberry, caramel or chocolate ice cream topping.
- Top each cupcake with a small scoop of ice cream, sorbet, sherbet or frozen yogurt. Add a drizzle of maple syrup, if desired.

Decorating Cupcakes

Once the cupcakes are frosted or glazed, you can add all kinds of toppings and decorations. The garnish you choose should partner well with the cupcake and the frosting, especially if it has a distinctive flavor. A chocolate candy, for instance, makes a lovely garnish, but it may not be as welcome on a pumpkin cupcake as a sprinkling of toasted pecans would be. Here are a few ideas for decorating frosted or glazed cupcakes:

- **Sprinkles:** Sprinkles come in many shapes and colors. Head to a craft store or cake decorating supply shop and choose from a variety of coarse or sanding sugars, small shapes, shimmer dust, pearls, nonpareils, jimmies and more.
- **Baking chips:** When it comes to baking chips, there's the old standby of semisweet chocolate chips, of course, but you can also choose milk chocolate, dark chocolate, white chocolate or mint chocolate. Other flavors include vanilla, butterscotch, cinnamon and peanut butter. Your final decision: mini or regular-size?
- **Chocolate curls:** To make chocolate curls, use a vegetable peeler to scrape the side of a plain chocolate bar or a bar of baking chocolate (dark, bittersweet, milk or white). You will find that cooler chocolate bars make shorter and smaller curls, while warmer bars make longer, more elegant curls. After a little practice, you will be a pro.
- **Candies:** There are so many options: mini candies, cinnamon hearts, candy-coated chocolates, jelly beans, candy corn, chocolate stars, lemon drops, conversation hearts … the list could go on and on. Stroll down the candy aisle and let your creativity soar. Larger sweets — such as peppermints, candy canes, chocolate peanut butter cups or whole candy bars — can be easily crushed or chopped to fit.
- **Nuts:** Anything goes — use whole nuts, chopped toasted nuts, slivers, pecan or walnut halves or honey-roasted peanuts. Stick with a single type or try a combination of different nuts.
- **Cookie or graham wafer crumbs:** Any cookie can be quickly crushed into crumbs in a food processor. Or place cookies in a sealable food

storage bag, seal and crush them with a rolling pin. Of course, if you get lucky, you might find packages of pre-crushed cookie crumbs at the grocery store.

- **Citrus fruits:** Grated zest, curls (just use a vegetable peeler to peel narrow strips) or thin slices of fruit all make attractive garnishes. When grating zest or cutting curls, avoid the white pith underneath the colored portion — it is quite bitter. Drained canned mandarin oranges are perfectly sized for our small cupcakes.

- **Berries:** Strawberries, raspberries, blueberries and other fresh berries make refreshing decorations. Use whole small berries or cut larger ones in half.

- **Other fresh fruits:** Fresh fruit options range from finely chopped fresh pineapple to pitted fresh cherries to sliced apples and pears. Remember, though, that certain fruits (including apples, pears and bananas) discolor very quickly once sliced, and although the fruit hasn't spoiled, the browned slices are not visually appealing. To help prolong the fresh appearance and color, dip the fruit in lemon juice as you slice it. Even then, these fruits should only be used when you intend to serve the cupcakes immediately.

- **Dried and candied fruits:** Chopped dried fruits, such as cranberries and apricots, and candied fruits, such as cherries and pineapple, are readily available and make ideal garnishes.

- **Mint leaves:** Choose fresh mint leaves that show no signs of wilting. Use small whole leaves, and add them just before serving so they do not wilt.

- **Edible flowers:** For a pretty garnish, choose edible flowers such as daisies, geraniums, lavender, marigolds, violets, pansies and roses. Be sure they are labeled "edible" and have not been sprayed with chemicals or pesticides. Not all flowers are edible; if in doubt, check with your local poison control center. You might use the entire bloom or snip off the leaves or petals. Add flowers just before serving so they look fresh and are at the peak of perfection.

- **Royal icing and gum paste:** Cake decorating supply shops and craft stores sell premade royal icing or gum paste decorations in many different sizes, shapes and colors. These days, in addition to the traditional designs, such as flowers and stars, you can also find decorations in the shape of animals, cartoon characters and sports gear — there's something for any holiday, event or theme.

- **Fondant:** Fondant is a flexible, sugar-based product. Because it is so pliable, it can be draped or formed into hundreds of different shapes. Many commercially available packages come already tinted in a variety of colors, but you can also add colored gel or paste to white fondant and knead it until it is evenly colored. To form shapes, first roll out the kneaded fondant on a board that is lightly coated with confectioners' (icing) sugar or cornstarch. Cut it into the desired shapes using a cookie cutter (or the tip of a sharp knife for tiny pieces). You can leave the fondant smooth or add an interesting texture by embossing it with rollers. Store fondant in an airtight container, as it dries out quickly.

- **Place card holders:** Write each guest's name on a small card and insert the corner of the card in the cupcake. You could even make cupcakes that match the other table decorations.

Flavored Butters for Muffins, Biscuits and Scones

A warm muffin, biscuit or scone tastes even better when it's split and spread with butter and maybe a dollop of preserves or jam. Or you can simply serve a flavored butter. Here are four easy recipes:

Tex-Mex Butter

In a small bowl, combine ¼ cup (60 mL) softened unsalted butter, 1 tbsp (15 mL) minced fresh cilantro, 1 tsp (5 mL) ground cumin and a pinch each of salt, freshly ground black pepper and garlic powder.

This butter is especially good on Cheese and Jalapeño Corn Muffins (page 110).

Citrus Butter

In a small bowl, combine ¼ cup (60 mL) softened salted butter, ½ tsp (2 mL) grated citrus zest and 1½ tsp (7 mL) freshly squeezed citrus juice.

This popular flavored butter is great on so many muffins. Match the citrus fruit you choose with the muffin. For example, serve orange butter with Orange Streusel Muffins (page 102) or top Lemon-Glazed Muffins (page 101) with lemon butter. You can also mix it up a bit and serve lemon butter on Blueberry Muffins (page 105) or a zesty lime butter on Honey Nut Muffins (page 98).

Honey Butter

In a small bowl, combine ¼ cup (60 mL) softened salted butter with 1½ tsp to 1 tbsp (7 to 15 mL) liquid honey. If desired, add 1 tbsp (15 mL) finely chopped toasted pecans or a pinch of ground cinnamon or ginger.

Serve honey butter with Honey Nut Muffins (page 98) or Apple Harvest Muffins (page 104).

Springtime Strawberry Butter

In a small bowl, combine ¼ cup (60 mL) softened unsalted butter with ¼ cup (60 mL) chopped strawberries.

Try this butter on Buttermilk Spice Tea Room Muffins (page 96).

Displaying Babycakes

You can have just as much fun deciding how to display your Babycakes as you did baking and decorating them! If you're throwing a theme party, make sure to follow through on the theme when selecting platters and other display pieces. Here are some classic presentation ideas:

- Purchase an inexpensive tiered display stand. Or use a pedestal cake stand for a professional look — stacking two or three stands together would be glamorous.

- Drape a cloth over arranged boxes so that platters of Babycakes can be set at different heights. Or use upside-down bowls as stands for your platters.

- Serve cupcakes or muffins from baskets.

- Place each decorated cupcake in an antique tea cup with saucer.

- Place decorated cupcakes on mirrors for a stunning display.

- Arrange lines of cupcakes on a sleek tabletop for a dramatic look.

- Accessorize your display with fabrics, ribbons, doilies, leaves, beads, garland, candies, candles or other decorative pieces.

Theme Party Cupcakes

What's more fun than a theme party, whether it's for the young or the young at heart? Here are some great ideas for cupcakes to match your theme.

Picnic Time

Frost cupcakes with green frosting and nestle gummy candy bugs or little bugs shaped from fondant in the frosting.

Garden Party

Create sunflowers by frosting cupcakes with bright yellow frosting. Place mini chocolate chips in the centers and arrange candy corn, pointed side out, in rings around the outer edges of the cupcakes.

Take Me Out to the Ball Game

Frost cupcakes with white frosting. Use red gel frosting or strips of red shoestring licorice to create arched stripes that resemble a baseball's stitches.

Final Four Basketball Frenzy

Frost cupcakes with brown frosting or caramel icing. Use black decorating gel with a fine writing tip or a piping bag of black frosting to pipe black stripes that resemble a basketball's pattern.

World Cup Cupcakes

Frost cupcakes with white frosting and use black decorating gel with a fine writing tip or a piping bag of black frosting to pipe black stripes that resemble a soccer ball's pattern.

Over the Hill

Wrap small boxes in black paper and arrange them on a serving table to create a set of stairs. Frost most of the cupcakes in black frosting and set them close together on the boxes. Frost a few cupcakes with white frosting and place them at the very top of the "hill," to create a snowcapped mountain.

Mardi Gras Party

Frost some cupcakes with purple frosting, some with green and some with yellow or gold. Top with sprinkles or sanding sugar for an elegant effect. Set Mardi Gras masks and beads nearby, then *laissez les bon temps roulez*.

Tea Party

No matter what your age, bake Princess Pink Party Cupcakes (page 37) or Pink Lemonade Cupcakes (page 47) and serve them on your best china. Serve with tea and Pimento Cheese Cups (page 160), and enjoy a complete tea service.

Pirate Party

Bake yellow or chocolate cupcakes and frost with gold-colored frosting. Sprinkle with golden edible glitter or gold sanding sugar. Fill a toy pirate chest with strings of plastic beads and gold-foil-wrapped chocolate coins, then nestle the golden cupcakes in the beads.

Out of This World Spaceship Party

Follow the directions for the Halloween Spooktaculars (page 202), making ghosts and Martians. Change the ghosts to spaceships by tinting the frosting gray and omitting the eyes and mouths. Surround the spaceships with green Martians.

Campfire Party

After the hot dogs are gobbled up, enjoy S'more Cupcakes (page 44).

Luau

Serve Tropical Muffins (page 107) with a salad, then indulge in Pineapple Cupcakes (page 49) for dessert.

Part 1

Cupcakes

Classic Anytime Cupcakes

Yellow Cupcakes

**Makes
26 to 28 cupcakes**

Yellow cupcakes with Chocolate Fudge Icing (page 92) are reminiscent of diner-style indulgences. Go back in time and enjoy these old-fashioned goodies. One of the best things about yellow cupcakes is that they are like little palettes, waiting for you to decorate or frost as you please.

Tips

No buttermilk on hand? Stir 1 1/2 tsp (7 mL) lemon juice or white vinegar into 1/2 cup (125 mL) milk. Let stand for 5 to 10 minutes or until thickened. Proceed with the recipe.

What to do with leftover egg whites? Cover and refrigerate them for up to 3 days. For longer storage, freeze them for up to 6 months (be sure to label and date each container). When you're ready to use them, let egg whites thaw in the refrigerator and use 2 tbsp (30 mL) for 1 egg white.

- Paper liners (optional)

1 1/4 cups	all-purpose flour	300 mL
1/2 tsp	baking powder	2 mL
1/4 tsp	baking soda	1 mL
1/4 tsp	salt	1 mL
3/4 cup	granulated sugar	175 mL
1	egg, at room temperature	1
1	egg yolk, at room temperature	1
1/2 cup	vegetable oil	125 mL
1 tsp	vanilla extract	5 mL
1/2 cup	buttermilk	125 mL

1. In a small bowl, whisk together flour, baking powder, baking soda and salt. Set aside.

2. In a large bowl, using an electric mixer on low speed, beat sugar, egg and egg yolk for 2 minutes or until thickened and a light cream color. Beat in oil and vanilla until blended. Add flour mixture alternately with buttermilk, making three additions of flour and two of buttermilk and beating until smooth.

3. If desired, place paper liners in wells. Fill each well with about 1 1/2 tbsp (22 mL) batter. Bake for 6 to 8 minutes or until a tester inserted in the center of a cupcake comes out clean. Transfer cupcakes to a wire rack to cool. Repeat with the remaining batter.

Vanilla Cupcakes

**Makes
16 to 20 cupcakes**

Why is it that some folks consider vanilla to be a plain and simple flavor? To some of us (like Kathy), vanilla is anything but bland.

Tips

Did you forget to set out the butter so that it will soften? Cut it into slices, place on a microwave-safe glass plate and microwave on Medium-Low (20%) for 10 to 15 seconds or until starting to soften. Let butter stand for about 10 minutes, then proceed with the recipe.

Separating an egg couldn't be easier. The recommended method is to pour the egg through an inexpensive egg separator, but if you don't have one, simply pour it into your hand, allowing the white to flow through your fingers and keeping the yolk in your hand.

- Paper liners (optional)

1 cup	all-purpose flour	250 mL
1 tsp	baking powder	5 mL
Pinch	salt	Pinch
¾ cup	granulated sugar	175 mL
⅓ cup	butter, softened	75 mL
¼ cup	sour cream	60 mL
3	egg whites, at room temperature	3
⅓ cup	milk	75 mL
2 tsp	vanilla extract	10 mL

1. In a small bowl, whisk together flour, baking powder and salt. Set aside.

2. In a medium bowl, using an electric mixer on medium-high speed, beat sugar and butter for 1 to 2 minutes or until fluffy. Beat in sour cream. Add egg whites and beat for 2 minutes, scraping the bowl occasionally. Add flour mixture alternately with milk, making three additions of flour and two of milk and beating on low speed until smooth. Stir in vanilla.

3. If desired, place paper liners in wells. Fill each well with about 1½ tbsp (22 mL) batter. Bake for 6 to 8 minutes or until a tester inserted in the center of a cupcake comes out clean. Transfer cupcakes to a wire rack to cool. Repeat with the remaining batter.

Chocolate Cupcakes

**Makes
22 to 24 cupcakes**

Here is the flip side to the chocolate or vanilla controversy. While Kathy picks vanilla as her favorite, Roxanne opts for chocolate. Neither is wrong. What is your favorite?

Tips

No buttermilk on hand? Stir 2 tsp (10 mL) lemon juice or white vinegar into 10 tbsp (150 mL) milk. Let stand for 5 to 10 minutes or until thickened. Proceed with the recipe.

Frost these cupcakes or dust them with confectioners' (icing) sugar. For added beauty and fun, make or purchase a small stencil and sift the confectioners' sugar over the stencil.

• Paper liners (optional)

1 oz	unsweetened chocolate, chopped	30 g
1 cup + 2 tbsp	all-purpose flour	280 mL
3 tbsp	unsweetened cocoa powder	45 mL
½ tsp	baking soda	2 mL
¼ tsp	baking powder	1 mL
¼ tsp	salt	1 mL
½ cup	granulated sugar	125 mL
⅓ cup	packed brown sugar	75 mL
¼ cup	butter, softened	60 mL
2	eggs, at room temperature	2
½ tsp	vanilla extract	2 mL
10 tbsp	buttermilk	150 mL

1. In a small microwave-safe glass bowl, microwave chocolate on High, in 30-second intervals, stirring after each, until melted. Let cool to room temperature.

2. In a medium bowl, whisk together flour, cocoa, baking soda, baking powder and salt. Set aside.

3. In a large bowl, using an electric mixer on medium-high speed, beat granulated sugar, brown sugar and butter for 1 to 2 minutes or until fluffy. Add eggs, one at a time, beating well after each addition. Stir in cooled chocolate and vanilla. Add flour mixture alternately with buttermilk, making three additions of flour and two of buttermilk and beating on low speed just until moistened (do not overbeat).

4. If desired, place paper liners in wells. Fill each well with about 1½ tbsp (22 mL) batter. Bake for 6 to 8 minutes or until a tester inserted in the center of a cupcake comes out clean. Transfer cupcakes to a wire rack to cool. Repeat with the remaining batter.

Chocolate Buttermilk Cupcakes

Makes 30 to 32 cupcakes

These will remind you of Grandma's cupcakes. The addition of hot brewed coffee intensifies the chocolate flavor.

Tips

This is an easy, old-fashioned, one-bowl cake. While the mixing method is different from the traditional method, the results are still moist and flavorful. You will enjoy the great flavor — and the fact that you only have one bowl to wash.

No buttermilk on hand? Stir 1½ tsp (7 mL) lemon juice or white vinegar into ½ cup (125 mL) milk. Let stand for 5 to 10 minutes or until thickened. Proceed with the recipe.

Prepare instant coffee according to package directions and substitute it for the brewed coffee.

You can frost these classic chocolate cupcakes with any favorite frosting.

• Paper liners (optional)

1 cup	all-purpose flour	250 mL
1 cup	granulated sugar	250 mL
½ cup	unsweetened cocoa powder	125 mL
1 tsp	baking soda	5 mL
½ tsp	baking powder	2 mL
½ tsp	salt	2 mL
1	egg, at room temperature	1
½ cup	buttermilk	125 mL
¼ cup	vegetable oil	60 mL
1 tsp	vanilla extract	5 mL
½ cup	hot brewed coffee	125 mL
	Creamy Chocolate Frosting (page 82)	

1. In a large bowl, whisk together flour, sugar, cocoa, baking soda, baking powder and salt.

2. Add egg, buttermilk, oil and vanilla to flour mixture and, using an electric mixer on medium speed, beat until blended and smooth. Using a wooden spoon, gently stir in coffee until mixture is smooth.

3. If desired, place paper liners in wells. Fill each well with about 1½ tbsp (22 mL) batter. Bake for 6 to 8 minutes or until a tester inserted in the center of a cupcake comes out clean. Transfer cupcakes to a wire rack to cool. Repeat with the remaining batter.

4. Frost with Creamy Chocolate Frosting.

German Chocolate Cupcakes

**Makes
28 to 30 cupcakes**

Sweet chocolate was developed by Sam German in the 1850s and is a little sweeter than semisweet chocolate. It was a very welcome change from the hard bricks of chocolate used by colonists of pre–Revolutionary War America to make a sweet chocolate drink. Any mention of the cake always makes one think of a mild, sweet chocolate cake topped with a coconut and pecan frosting — a cake made famous in the 1950s and the inspiration for these cupcakes.

Tips

You can substitute semisweet chocolate chips for the sweet chocolate.

No buttermilk on hand? Stir 1½ tsp (7 mL) lemon juice or white vinegar into ½ cup (125 mL) milk. Let stand for 5 to 10 minutes or until thickened. Proceed with the recipe.

• Paper liners

2 oz	sweet chocolate (such as Baker's German's or Baker's), chopped	60 g
¼ cup	water	60 mL
1 cup	all-purpose flour	250 mL
½ tsp	baking soda	2 mL
Pinch	salt	Pinch
1 cup	granulated sugar	250 mL
½ cup	butter, softened	125 mL
2	eggs, separated, at room temperature	2
1 tsp	vanilla extract	5 mL
½ cup	buttermilk	125 mL
	Coconut Pecan Frosting (page 85)	

1. In a small microwave-safe glass bowl, combine chocolate and water. Microwave on High for 30 to 40 seconds or until chocolate is almost melted. Stir until chocolate is completely melted. Set aside.

2. In a small bowl, whisk together flour, baking soda and salt. Set aside.

3. In a large bowl, using an electric mixer on medium-high speed, beat sugar and butter for 1 to 2 minutes or until fluffy. Add egg yolks, one at a time, beating well after each addition. Beat in melted chocolate and vanilla. Add flour mixture alternately with buttermilk, making three additions of flour and two of buttermilk and beating on low speed until blended.

4. In a small bowl, using an electric mixer with clean beaters, beat egg whites on high speed until stiff peaks form. Gently stir into batter, just until blended.

5. Place paper liners in wells. Fill each well with about 1½ tbsp (22 mL) batter. Bake for 6 to 8 minutes or until a tester inserted in the center of a cupcake comes out clean. Transfer cupcakes to a wire rack to cool. Repeat with the remaining batter.

6. Frost with Coconut Pecan Frosting.

Red Velvet Cupcakes

Many cupcake bakeries report that red velvet is one of the top-selling flavors. Now you can bake your own every day of the year!

Tips

If you don't have white vinegar, you can substitute cider vinegar in this recipe. Other vinegars, such as red wine vinegar or herb-flavored vinegars, will conflict in flavor and should not be used.

No buttermilk on hand? Stir 1½ tsp (7 mL) lemon juice or white vinegar into ½ cup (125 mL) milk. Let stand for 5 to 10 minutes or until thickened. Proceed with the recipe.

• Paper liners (optional)

1¼ cups	all-purpose flour	300 mL
4 tsp	unsweetened cocoa powder	20 mL
½ tsp	baking soda	2 mL
¼ tsp	baking powder	1 mL
¼ tsp	salt	1 mL
¾ cup	granulated sugar	175 mL
1	egg, at room temperature	1
¾ cup	vegetable oil	175 mL
1 tbsp	red food coloring	15 mL
½ tsp	vanilla extract	2 mL
½ cup	buttermilk	125 mL
½ tsp	white vinegar	2 mL
	Cream Cheese Frosting (page 90)	

1. In a small bowl, whisk together flour, cocoa, baking soda, baking powder and salt. Set aside.

2. In a large bowl, using an electric mixer on medium-high speed, beat sugar, egg and oil for 1 to 2 minutes or until fluffy. Beat in food coloring and vanilla. Add flour mixture alternately with buttermilk, making three additions of flour and two of buttermilk and beating on low speed until smooth. Stir in vinegar.

3. If desired, place paper liners in wells. Fill each well with about 1½ tbsp (22 mL) batter. Bake for 6 to 8 minutes or until a tester inserted in the center of a cupcake comes out clean. Transfer cupcakes to a wire rack to cool. Repeat with the remaining batter.

4. Frost with Cream Cheese Frosting.

Chocolate Chip Cupcakes

**Makes
20 to 22 cupcakes**

These two-bite treats
are festive, fun and
filled with flavor. Mini
chocolate chips are
the perfect size for
Babycakes!

Tip

No buttermilk on hand?
Stir 1 tsp (5 mL) lemon juice
or white vinegar into 1/3 cup
(75 mL) milk. Let stand for
5 to 10 minutes or until
thickened. Proceed with
the recipe.

Variation

Substitute regular-size
chocolate chips for the mini
chips, or use your favorite
flavor of baking chips, such
as cinnamon, butterscotch,
mint or vanilla.

● Paper liners (optional)

1 cup	all-purpose flour	250 mL
1 tsp	baking powder	5 mL
Pinch	salt	Pinch
1/2 cup	granulated sugar	125 mL
1/4 cup	butter, softened	60 mL
1	egg	1
1	egg yolk	1
1/3 cup	buttermilk	75 mL
1 tsp	vanilla extract	5 mL
1/4 cup	mini semisweet chocolate chips	60 mL

1. In a small bowl, whisk together flour, baking powder and salt. Set aside.

2. In a medium bowl, using an electric mixer on medium-high speed, beat sugar and butter for 1 to 2 minutes or until fluffy. Beat in egg and egg yolk. Beat in buttermilk and vanilla until smooth. Reduce mixer speed to low and beat in flour mixture until just blended. Fold in chocolate chips.

3. If desired, place paper liners in wells. Fill each well with about 1 1/2 tbsp (22 mL) batter. Bake for 6 to 8 minutes or until a tester inserted in the center of a cupcake comes out clean. Transfer cupcakes to a wire rack to cool. Repeat with the remaining batter.

Lemon Cupcakes

Lemon tastes refreshing no matter what time of year. We know it takes a minute to freshly squeeze the juice, but the flavor of the cupcakes will be so much better — you will be glad you did.

Tips

Top with Lemon Glaze (page 93) or frost with Lemon Buttercream Frosting (page 80) or Cream Cheese Frosting (page 90). Garnish with tiny curls of lemon zest, if desired.

For ease, zest the lemon first, then juice it. One lemon will yield about 3 tbsp (45 mL) juice and 2 to 3 tsp (10 to 15 mL) zest. Zest only the colored portion of the peel, avoiding the bitter white pith underneath. If you have leftover lemon juice, cover and refrigerate it for up to 5 days, or freeze it for up to 6 months.

- Paper liners (optional)

1 cup	all-purpose flour	250 mL
1 tsp	baking powder	5 mL
1/2 tsp	baking soda	2 mL
Pinch	salt	Pinch
3/4 cup	granulated sugar	175 mL
1/3 cup	butter, softened	75 mL
2	eggs, at room temperature	2
1/4 cup	sour cream	60 mL
	Grated zest of 1 lemon	
3 tbsp	freshly squeezed lemon juice	45 mL
3 tbsp	milk	45 mL
1/2 tsp	lemon extract (optional)	2 mL

1. In a small bowl, whisk together flour, baking powder, baking soda and salt. Set aside.

2. In a medium bowl, using an electric mixer on medium-high speed, beat sugar and butter for 1 to 2 minutes or until fluffy. Add eggs, one at a time, beating well after each addition. Beat in sour cream and lemon zest. Reduce mixer speed to low and beat in one-third of the flour mixture. Beat in lemon juice, then another third of the flour mixture, then milk. Beat in the remaining flour mixture. Stir in lemon extract (if using).

3. If desired, place paper liners in wells. Fill each well with about 1 1/2 tbsp (22 mL) batter. Bake for 6 to 8 minutes or until a tester inserted in the center of a cupcake comes out clean. Transfer cupcakes to a wire rack to cool. Repeat with the remaining batter.

Orange Blossom Cupcakes

**Makes
32 to 36 cupcakes**

Citrus blossoms
are delicate and yet
unfold to offer such
vibrancy. The same
might be said for these
cupcakes, which offer
a delicate first bite
followed by lots of
flavor depth.

Tip

A rasp grater, such as a
Microplane, is the perfect
tool for grating citrus zest.
Wash the fruit and pat it dry,
then grate it with the rasp
using a light motion. For
the best flavor, grate only
the colored portion of the
peel, avoiding the bitter
white pith underneath. The
fine side of a box cheese
grater is a good alternative
to a rasp.

• Paper liners (optional)

1 1/2 cups	all-purpose flour	375 mL
1 1/2 tsp	baking powder	7 mL
Pinch	salt	Pinch
3/4 cup	granulated sugar	175 mL
1/3 cup	butter, softened	75 mL
2	eggs, at room temperature	2
1 tsp	grated orange zest	5 mL
1/2 cup	freshly squeezed orange juice	125 mL
1/3 cup	milk	75 mL
1/2 tsp	vanilla extract	2 mL
1/4 tsp	orange extract	1 mL
	Orange Blossom Buttercream Frosting (page 81)	

1. In a medium bowl, whisk together flour, baking powder and salt. Set aside.

2. In a large bowl, using an electric mixer on medium-high speed, beat sugar and butter for 1 to 2 minutes or until fluffy. Add eggs, one at a time, beating well after each addition. Beat in orange zest. Reduce mixer speed to low and beat in one-third of the flour mixture. Beat in orange juice, then another third of the flour mixture, then milk. Beat in the remaining flour mixture. Stir in vanilla and orange extract.

3. If desired, place paper liners in wells. Fill each well with about 1 1/2 tbsp (22 mL) batter. Bake for 6 to 8 minutes or until a tester inserted in the center of a cupcake comes out clean. Transfer cupcakes to a wire rack to cool. Repeat with the remaining batter.

4. Frost with Orange Blossom Buttercream Frosting.

Strawberry Cupcakes

Roxanne's family participates in game night each month with the Bell and Stapp families. Both kids and adults enjoy playing such games as mah-jong and charades. Of course, no game night would be complete without treats. Cayce Stapp requests these cupcakes each and every month, without fail. This one's for you, Cayce.

Tips

Frost these luscious cupcakes with Strawberry Frosting (page 84), if desired.

Ten tablespoons is equal to $\frac{1}{2}$ cup + 2 tbsp, if you find it easier to measure the water that way.

- Paper liners (optional)

2 cups	white cake mix	500 mL
2	eggs, at room temperature	2
$\frac{1}{2}$ cup	frozen halved strawberries in syrup, thawed	125 mL
10 tbsp	water	150 mL
$\frac{1}{4}$ cup	vegetable oil	60 mL

1. In a medium bowl, using an electric mixer on low speed, beat cake mix, eggs, strawberries, water and oil for 30 seconds or until moistened. Beat on medium speed for 2 minutes.

2. If desired, place paper liners in wells. Fill each well with about $1\frac{1}{2}$ tbsp (22 mL) batter. Bake for 6 to 8 minutes or until a tester inserted in the center of a cupcake comes out clean. Transfer cupcakes to a wire rack to cool. Repeat with the remaining batter.

Butter Pecan Cupcakes

Some would say that anything is better with a bit of butter. Add toasted pecans as well, and cake mix goes from everyday to really special. We'd like to dedicate this recipe to Kathy's dad, because he thought there was no finer flavor combination than butter and pecans.

Tip

Toasting pecans intensifies their flavor. Spread chopped pecans in a single layer on a baking sheet. Bake at 350°F (180°C) for 5 to 7 minutes or until lightly browned. Let cool, then measure.

• Paper liners (optional)

2 cups	yellow cake mix	500 mL
2	eggs, at room temperature	2
½ cup	milk	125 mL
¼ cup	butter, melted	60 mL
1 tsp	vanilla extract	5 mL
¼ cup	finely chopped pecans, toasted (see tip, at left)	60 mL
	Praline Frosting (page 83)	

1. In a medium bowl, using an electric mixer on low speed, beat cake mix, eggs, milk, butter and vanilla for 30 seconds or until moistened. Beat on medium speed for 2 minutes. Stir in pecans.

2. If desired, place paper liners in wells. Fill each well with about 1½ tbsp (22 mL) batter. Bake for 6 to 8 minutes or until a tester inserted in the center of a cupcake comes out clean. Transfer cupcakes to a wire rack to cool. Repeat with the remaining batter.

3. Frost with Praline Frosting.

Spice Cupcakes

While some may think of spices such as ginger and cloves as flavors for fall or for holidays, this cupcake really is a year-round favorite. The enticing aroma will remind you of being in Grandma's kitchen.

Tip

Spice cupcakes are excellent with Cream Cheese Frosting (page 90) or Caramel Frosting (page 82). We were both born in Missouri, where fried apples are a favorite, so we love to spoon fried apples on top of the frosted cupcakes. (To make fried apples, sauté apple slices in a little butter, then stir in some granulated sugar and ground cinnamon and cook until apples are tender.) You could also use a dollop of apple butter.

• Paper liners (optional)

1¾ cups	all-purpose flour	425 mL
1 tsp	baking powder	5 mL
1 tsp	ground cinnamon	5 mL
¼ tsp	baking soda	1 mL
¼ tsp	salt	1 mL
¼ tsp	ground cloves	1 mL
¼ tsp	ground ginger	1 mL
¾ cup	granulated sugar	175 mL
⅓ cup	packed brown sugar	75 mL
6 tbsp	butter, softened	90 mL
2	eggs, at room temperature	2
1 tsp	vanilla extract	5 mL
¾ cup	milk	175 mL

1. In a medium bowl, whisk together flour, baking powder, cinnamon, baking soda, salt, cloves and ginger. Set aside.

2. In a large bowl, using an electric mixer on medium-high speed, beat granulated sugar, brown sugar and butter for 1 to 2 minutes or until fluffy. Add eggs, one at a time, beating well after each addition. Beat in vanilla. Add flour mixture alternately with milk, making three additions of flour and two of milk and beating on low speed until smooth.

3. If desired, place paper liners in wells. Fill each well with about 1½ tbsp (22 mL) batter. Bake for 6 to 8 minutes or until a tester inserted in the center of a cupcake comes out clean. Transfer cupcakes to a wire rack to cool. Repeat with the remaining batter.

Gingerbread Cupcakes

**Makes
16 to 18 cupcakes**

This recipe is one of Kathy's year-round favorites. Sure, make these cupcakes during the holidays, but why stop there? Enjoy them any day.

Tips

Gingerbread cupcakes are especially good when frosted with Lemon Buttercream Frosting (page 80).

Molasses comes from boiling the juice that is extracted from processing sugar cane or beets into sugar. Light (fancy) and dark (cooking) molasses can be used interchangeably in this recipe, but dark molasses will give a more robust flavor.

- Paper liners (optional)

1 cup	all-purpose flour	250 mL
1 tsp	baking powder	5 mL
1 tsp	ground ginger	5 mL
1/2 tsp	baking soda	2 mL
1/2 tsp	ground cinnamon	2 mL
1/4 tsp	ground cloves	1 mL
Pinch	salt	Pinch
1/4 cup	packed brown sugar	60 mL
1/4 cup	butter, softened	60 mL
2 tbsp	light (white or golden) corn syrup	30 mL
2 tbsp	unsulfured dark (cooking) molasses	30 mL
1	egg, at room temperature, lightly beaten	1
1/3 cup	milk	75 mL

1. In a medium bowl, whisk together flour, baking powder, ginger, baking soda, cinnamon, cloves and salt. Set aside.

2. In a small saucepan, combine brown sugar, butter, corn syrup and molasses; heat over low heat, stirring frequently, for about 3 minutes or until butter has melted and sugar has dissolved. Pour over flour mixture. Stir in egg and milk until blended.

3. If desired, place paper liners in wells. Fill each well with about 1 1/2 tbsp (22 mL) batter. Bake for 6 to 8 minutes or until a tester inserted in the center of a cupcake comes out clean. Transfer cupcakes to a wire rack to cool. Repeat with the remaining batter.

Carrot Cupcakes

These carrot cupcakes are moist and wonderful. It is easy to shred the carrots using a food processor, but if you're short on time, look for shredded carrots on the salad bar at your local grocery store.

Tips

Toasting pecans intensifies their flavor. Spread chopped pecans in a single layer on a baking sheet. Bake at 350°F (180°C) for 5 to 7 minutes or until lightly browned. Let cool, then measure.

Carrot cupcakes are especially good with Cream Cheese Frosting (page 90).

• Paper liners (optional)

1 cup	all-purpose flour	250 mL
1 tsp	baking powder	5 mL
1 tsp	ground cinnamon	5 mL
¼ tsp	baking soda	1 mL
¼ tsp	salt	1 mL
1¼ cups	shredded carrots (about 3 medium)	300 mL
½ cup	chopped pecans, toasted (see tip, at left)	125 mL
¾ cup	granulated sugar	175 mL
2	eggs, at room temperature	2
½ cup	vegetable oil	125 mL
1 tsp	vanilla extract	5 mL

1. In a medium bowl, whisk together flour, baking powder, cinnamon, baking soda and salt. Stir in carrots and pecans, tossing lightly to coat. Set aside.

2. In a large bowl, using an electric mixer on medium speed, beat sugar, eggs, oil and vanilla for 1 minute or until light-colored. Using a wooden spoon, stir in flour mixture until blended.

3. If desired, place paper liners in wells. Fill each well with about 1½ tbsp (22 mL) batter. Bake for 6 to 8 minutes or until a tester inserted in the center of a cupcake comes out clean. Transfer cupcakes to a wire rack to cool. Repeat with the remaining batter.

Pumpkin Cupcakes

Each and every fall, Kathy's family attends at least one University of Missouri football game. These cupcakes are always packed for the drive and for the tailgate festivities. Her family usually has to toss a coin to see who gets the last one!

Tips

These cupcakes are also good without the pecans, if you prefer.

Leftover canned pumpkin purée? Refrigerate it in an airtight container for up to 1 week, or freeze it for up to 3 months. To use from frozen, thaw the pumpkin overnight in the refrigerator, then stir well and use it to bake another batch of cupcakes.

Variation

Chocolate lovers can add 1/4 cup (60 mL) mini semisweet chocolate chips with the pecans.

- Paper liners (optional)

1¾ cups	all-purpose flour	425 mL
2 tsp	baking powder	10 mL
2 tsp	pumpkin pie spice	10 mL
¼ tsp	baking soda	1 mL
¼ tsp	salt	1 mL
1 cup	granulated sugar	250 mL
⅓ cup	butter, softened	75 mL
2	eggs, at room temperature	2
¾ cup	canned pumpkin purée (not pie filling)	175 mL
½ cup	milk	125 mL
⅓ cup	chopped pecans, toasted (see tip, page 33)	75 mL

1. In a medium bowl, whisk together flour, baking powder, pumpkin pie spice, baking soda and salt. Set aside.

2. In a large bowl, using an electric mixer on medium-high speed, beat sugar and butter for 1 to 2 minutes or until fluffy. Add eggs, one at a time, beating well after each addition. Beat in pumpkin purée. Add flour mixture alternately with milk, making three additions of flour and two of milk and beating on low speed until smooth. Stir in pecans.

3. If desired, place paper liners in wells. Fill each well with about 1½ tbsp (22 mL) batter. Bake for 6 to 8 minutes or until a tester inserted in the center of a cupcake comes out clean. Transfer cupcakes to a wire rack to cool. Repeat with the remaining batter.

Kid Favorites

Confetti Cupcakes

**Makes
30 to 34 cupcakes**

Every child has an all-time favorite cupcake they like to share with friends. Roxanne's daughter, Grace, rates this as her first pick for school parties.

Tips

Frost with Buttercream Frosting (page 80) or Chocolate Fudge Icing (page 92).

No buttermilk on hand? Stir 1½ tsp (7 mL) lemon juice or white vinegar into ½ cup (125 mL) milk. Let stand for 5 to 10 minutes or until thickened. Proceed with the recipe.

Variation

Substitute white cake mix or strawberry cake mix for the French vanilla cake mix.

• Paper liners (optional)

2 cups	French vanilla cake mix	500 mL
2	egg whites, at room temperature	2
1	egg, at room temperature	1
½ cup	buttermilk	125 mL
¼ cup	vegetable oil	60 mL
½ tsp	vanilla extract	2 mL
2 tbsp	sprinkles	30 mL

1. In a large bowl, using an electric mixer on low speed, beat cake mix, egg whites, egg, buttermilk, oil and vanilla for 30 seconds or until moistened. Beat on medium speed for 2 minutes. Gently stir in sprinkles.

2. If desired, place paper liners in wells. Fill each well with about 1½ tbsp (22 mL) batter. Bake for 6 to 8 minutes or until a tester inserted in the center of a cupcake comes out clean. Transfer cupcakes to a wire rack to cool. Repeat with the remaining batter.

Princess Pink Party Cupcakes

These pink morsels will be the hit of the princess party. Sprinkle with pink sugar for added sparkle. In fact, princesses of any age will be happy to indulge in these treats.

Tips

Vary the color and flavor of the cupcakes by selecting a different flavor of gelatin, such as orange or blueberry. Be sure to use a matching or complementary frosting color.

Seal leftover flavored gelatin in a sealable plastic bag, label and store in the cupboard for up to 3 months.

- Paper liners (optional)

1/4 cup	butter, softened	60 mL
1 cup	all-purpose flour	250 mL
1/2 cup	granulated sugar	125 mL
3 tbsp	strawberry-flavored gelatin powder	45 mL
1/2 tsp	baking soda	2 mL
1/2 tsp	baking powder	2 mL
1/4 tsp	salt	1 mL
1	egg, at room temperature	1
1/3 cup	sour cream	75 mL
1/4 cup	milk	60 mL
1/2 tsp	vanilla extract	2 mL
	Buttercream Frosting (page 80), tinted pink	

1. In a large bowl, using an electric mixer on medium-high speed, beat butter for 1 to 2 minutes or until fluffy. Add flour, sugar, gelatin, baking soda, baking powder, salt, egg, sour cream, milk and vanilla; beat for 1 to 2 minutes or until smooth.

2. If desired, place paper liners in wells. Fill each well with about 1 1/2 tbsp (22 mL) batter. Bake for 6 to 8 minutes or until a tester inserted in the center of a cupcake comes out clean. Transfer cupcakes to a wire rack to cool. Repeat with the remaining batter.

3. Frost with pink Buttercream Frosting.

Triple Chocolate Cupcakes

Just say chocolate to some people and their mouths water. Tell them this wonderful cupcake is packed with three different kinds of chocolate and watch the excitement build.

Tips

To melt unsweetened chocolate squares, place chocolate in a small microwave-safe glass bowl and microwave on High in 30-second intervals, stirring after each, until melted. Let cool slightly.

Frost with Creamy Chocolate Frosting (page 82) or Buttercream Frosting (page 80).

No buttermilk on hand? Stir 2 tsp (10 mL) lemon juice or white vinegar into ¾ cup (175 mL) milk. Let stand for 5 to 10 minutes or until thickened. Proceed with the recipe.

• Paper liners (optional)

1 cup	all-purpose flour	250 mL
¼ cup	unsweetened cocoa powder	60 mL
½ tsp	baking powder	2 mL
½ tsp	baking soda	2 mL
¼ tsp	salt	1 mL
½ cup	granulated sugar	125 mL
¼ cup	packed brown sugar	60 mL
½ cup	butter, softened	125 mL
2	eggs, at room temperature	2
2 oz	unsweetened chocolate, melted (see tip, at left)	60 g
1 tsp	vanilla extract	5 mL
¾ cup	buttermilk	175 mL
¼ cup	mini semisweet chocolate chips	60 mL

1. In a small bowl, whisk together flour, cocoa, baking powder, baking soda and salt. Set aside.

2. In a medium bowl, using an electric mixer on medium-high speed, beat granulated sugar, brown sugar and butter for 1 to 2 minutes or until fluffy. Add eggs, one at a time, beating well after each addition. Beat in melted chocolate and vanilla. Add flour mixture alternately with buttermilk, making three additions of flour and two of buttermilk and beating on low speed until smooth. Gently stir in chocolate chips.

3. If desired, place paper liners in wells. Fill each well with about 1½ tbsp (22 mL) batter. Bake for 6 to 8 minutes or until a tester inserted in the center of a cupcake comes out clean. Transfer cupcakes to a wire rack to cool. Repeat with the remaining batter.

Cookies and Cream Cupcakes

**Makes
30 to 32 cupcakes**

Each year, we work at a large trade show that showcases the latest and greatest in appliances and kitchen items. We served these fun cupcakes at one of those shows. Believe us when we say these are a favorite for kids of all ages!

Tip

When separating the chocolate sandwich cookies, don't worry if the cream filling divides unevenly between the two wafers. In this recipe, it doesn't matter — all of the cupcakes will taste great.

- Paper liners

25	cream-filled chocolate sandwich cookies	25
2 cups	white cake mix	500 mL
2	eggs, at room temperature	2
1/2 cup	water	125 mL
1/4 cup	vegetable oil	60 mL
2 tbsp	milk	30 mL
1 tsp	vanilla extract	5 mL
	Buttercream Frosting (page 80)	

1. Separate 16 of the cookies into two single wafers (see tip, at left). Set aside.

2. Place the remaining 9 cookies in a sealable food storage bag and, using a rolling pin or a mallet, crush into coarse crumbs. Measure out $\frac{2}{3}$ cup (150 mL) crumbs; reserve the remaining crumbs separately.

3. In a medium bowl, using an electric mixer on low speed, beat cake mix, eggs, water, oil, milk and vanilla for 30 seconds or until moistened. Beat on medium speed for 2 minutes. Gently stir in the $\frac{2}{3}$ cup (150 mL) cookie crumbs.

4. Place paper liners in wells. Place one half-cookie, cream side up, in each liner. Fill each well with about $1\frac{1}{2}$ tbsp (22 mL) batter. Bake for 6 to 8 minutes or until a tester inserted in the center of a cupcake comes out clean. Transfer cupcakes to a wire rack to cool. Repeat with the remaining batter.

5. Frost with Buttercream Frosting. Sprinkle with reserved cookie crumbs.

Hot Chocolate Cupcakes

Who doesn't think of a cup of hot chocolate on a cold winter evening? The Kansas City area has a large fireworks display the night before Thanksgiving, and it is always a very cold night. Roxanne brings hot chocolate when our families meet to watch the fireworks.

These cute little cupcakes, made with hot chocolate drink mix and decorated to look like mugs of hot chocolate, remind us of those fun chilly evenings.

Tip

Did you forget to set out the butter so that it will soften? Cut it into slices, place on a microwave-safe glass plate and microwave on Medium-Low (20%) for 10 to 15 seconds or until starting to soften. Let butter stand for about 10 minutes, then proceed with the recipe.

• Paper liners (optional)

¾ cup	butter, softened	175 mL
¾ cup	milk	175 mL
2	envelopes (each 1 oz/30 g) hot chocolate drink mix (see tip, at right)	2
1½ cups	all-purpose flour	375 mL
¾ cup	granulated sugar	175 mL
2 tbsp	unsweetened cocoa powder	30 mL
1½ tsp	baking powder	7 mL
¼ tsp	salt	1 mL
2	eggs, at room temperature	2
1 tsp	vanilla extract	5 mL
	Marshmallow Frosting (page 84)	
78 to 84	mini marshmallows	78 to 84
13 to 14	mini pretzel twists, broken in half	13 to 14
	Chocolate sundae syrup (optional)	

1. In a small saucepan, combine butter and milk; heat over medium heat, stirring frequently, for about 6 minutes or until butter is melted (do not let boil). Remove from heat and let cool slightly.

2. In a large bowl, whisk together hot chocolate drink mix, flour, sugar, cocoa, baking powder and salt. Add butter mixture, eggs and vanilla; using an electric mixer on low speed, beat for 30 seconds or until blended and smooth. Beat on medium speed for 1 minute.

Tips

For this recipe, use the individual hot chocolate mix envelopes that are added to hot water or milk. Do not use those with marshmallows in the mix.

If desired, omit the pretzels.

Instead of the chocolate syrup drizzle, sprinkle the tops very lightly with unsweetened cocoa powder or ground nutmeg.

3. If desired, place paper liners in wells. Fill each well with about 1½ tbsp (22 mL) batter. Bake for 6 to 8 minutes or until a tester inserted in the center of a cupcake comes out clean. Transfer cupcakes to a wire rack to cool. Repeat with the remaining batter.

4. Frost with Marshmallow Frosting.

5. Place 3 mini marshmallows on top of each cupcake. Use a tiny bit of frosting as glue and secure half a pretzel twist to the side of each cupcake to resemble a handle on a mug. Garnish the top of each cupcake with a light drizzle of chocolate syrup, if desired.

Chocolate Peanut Butter Cupcakes

Makes
30 to 34 cupcakes

Kathy's daughter Amanda is the chocolate–peanut butter lover of all time. She adores these cupcakes — and she'll vouch for the fact that you don't have to be a child to enjoy this classic flavor combo.

Tips

Ten tablespoons is equal to 1/2 cup + 2 tbsp, if you find it easier to measure the water that way.

If desired, omit the chopped chocolate peanut butter cup candies and sprinkle the tops with chopped dry-roasted peanuts or small candy-coated peanut butter candies.

• Paper liners (optional)

2 cups	milk chocolate cake mix	500 mL
2	eggs, at room temperature	2
10 tbsp	water	150 mL
1/3 cup	creamy peanut butter	75 mL
3 tbsp	vegetable oil	45 mL
	Peanut Butter Cream Cheese Frosting (page 90)	
1/2 cup	chopped chocolate peanut butter cup candies (about 4 snack-size)	125 mL
	Chocolate Drizzle (page 92)	

1. In a large bowl, using an electric mixer on low speed, beat cake mix, eggs, water, peanut butter and oil for 30 seconds or until moistened. Beat on medium speed for 2 minutes.

2. If desired, place paper liners in wells. Fill each well with about 1 1/2 tbsp (22 mL) batter. Bake for 6 to 8 minutes or until a tester inserted in the center of a cupcake comes out clean. Transfer cupcakes to a wire rack to cool. Repeat with the remaining batter.

3. Frost with Peanut Butter Cream Cheese Frosting. Arrange candies on top, then drizzle with Chocolate Drizzle.

PB&J Snack Cakes

**Makes
34 to 36 cupcakes**

The old standby of peanut butter and jelly gets a makeover as a Babycakes delight. Kids old and young will enjoy these tiny cakes stuffed with grape jelly.

Tips

If you prefer a lot of frosting on your cupcakes, you will need to double the recipe for the Peanut Butter Cream Cheese Frosting.

The cake you cut from the tops of these cupcakes may be reserved for other uses. Try layering the cake pieces with fresh fruit for a parfait, or crumbling them over ice cream. Freeze leftover cake in a freezer bag for up to 2 months.

Variation

Use your favorite jelly, such as strawberry or apricot.

- Paper liners (optional)
- Icing bag fitted with a #12 (or small plain) decorating tip

1	box (16 oz/500 g) pound cake mix	1
	Eggs, oil and water as called for on cake mix package	
½ cup	grape jelly	125 mL
	Peanut Butter Cream Cheese Frosting (page 90)	

1. Prepare pound cake mix according to package directions.

2. If desired, place paper liners in wells. Fill each well with about 1½ tbsp (22 mL) batter. Bake for 6 to 8 minutes or until a tester inserted in the center of a cupcake comes out clean. Transfer cupcakes to a wire rack to cool. Repeat with the remaining batter.

3. Using a serrated knife, carefully cut a ½-inch (1 cm) circle or indentation from the top center of each cupcake (see tip, at left).

4. Place grape jelly in a sealable food storage bag, seal and cut the tip off a corner. Fill each circle with grape jelly.

5. Fill icing bag with frosting and pipe over each cupcake, covering jelly.

S'more Cupcakes

These are perfect for indoor overnights when there is not a campfire to be had, yet elegant enough to be served at a fancy dinner party. Roxanne's husband, Bob, voted them his favorite cupcakes of all.

Tips

Instead of using an icing bag, you can just fill a sealable food storage bag with frosting, seal it and cut the tip off a corner.

Separating an egg couldn't be easier. The recommended method is to pour the egg through an inexpensive egg separator, but if you don't have one, simply pour it into your hand, allowing the white to flow through your fingers and keeping the yolk in your hand.

What to do with leftover egg whites? Cover and refrigerate them for up to 3 days. For longer storage, freeze them for up to 6 months (be sure to label and date each container). When you're ready to use them, let egg whites thaw in the refrigerator and use 2 tbsp (30 mL) for 1 egg white.

- Paper liners
- Icing bag fitted with a #12 (or small plain) decorating tip (see tip, at left)

Cupcakes

1¼ cups	all-purpose flour	300 mL
1¼ tsp	baking powder	6 mL
½ tsp	salt	2 mL
¾ cup	granulated sugar	175 mL
½ cup	butter, softened	125 mL
1	egg, at room temperature	1
1	egg yolk, at room temperature	1
1 tsp	vanilla extract	5 mL
½ cup	milk	125 mL
½ cup	semisweet chocolate chips	125 mL
	Marshmallow Graham Frosting (variation, page 84)	

Topping

¼ cup	half-and-half (10%) cream	60 mL
1 cup	semisweet chocolate chips	250 mL
2 tbsp	graham wafer crumbs	30 mL

1. *Cupcakes:* In a small bowl, whisk together flour, baking powder and salt. Set aside.

2. In a large bowl, using an electric mixer on medium-high speed, beat sugar and butter for 1 to 2 minutes or until fluffy. Add egg and egg yolk, one at a time, beating well after each addition. Beat in vanilla. Add flour mixture alternately with milk, making three additions of flour and two of milk and beating on low speed until smooth. Gently stir in chocolate chips.

3. Place paper liners in wells. Fill each well with about 1½ tbsp (22 mL) batter. Bake for 6 to 8 minutes or until a tester inserted in the center of a cupcake comes out clean. Transfer cupcakes to a wire rack to cool. Repeat with the remaining batter.

Tips

If you prefer, you can use mini semisweet chocolate chips instead of the regular ones.

For a playful presentation, place a mini marshmallow in the center of the frosting on each cupcake after sprinkling with graham wafer crumbs.

4. Fill icing bag with frosting and pipe frosting onto each cupcake in a circular fashion, creating a top-hat look. Refrigerate cupcakes for 30 minutes.

5. *Topping:* In a microwave-safe glass bowl, microwave cream on High for 20 to 40 seconds, until it just comes to a boil (watch carefully to make sure it doesn't boil over). Add chocolate chips and stir until chips are melted and mixture is smooth.

6. Holding a cupcake firmly with the paper liner, carefully turn it upside down and dip its frosting cap into the topping. Place upright on a platter and repeat with the remaining cupcakes. Sprinkle cupcakes evenly with graham wafer crumbs.

Applesauce Cupcakes

**Makes
16 to 18 cupcakes**

Kathy's grandmother always made applesauce cake with caramel frosting as a special treat for Kathy and her sister when they came to visit. These miniature versions are our tribute to her.

Tips

An individual 4-oz (125 mL) serving of applesauce, the kind intended for lunchbox use, is perfect for this recipe because it doesn't create any waste or leftovers.

Toasting pecans intensifies their flavor. Spread chopped pecans in a single layer on a baking sheet. Bake at 350°F (180°C) for 5 to 7 minutes or until lightly browned. Let cool, then measure.

Variation

Frost with Cream Cheese Frosting (page 90), or dust with confectioners' (icing) sugar. Or simply eat the cupcakes plain!

- Paper liners (optional)

1 cup	all-purpose flour	250 mL
⅔ cup	packed brown sugar	150 mL
1 tsp	ground cinnamon	5 mL
½ tsp	baking soda	2 mL
¼ tsp	baking powder	1 mL
¼ tsp	salt	1 mL
½ cup	sweetened applesauce	125 mL
2 tbsp	vegetable oil	30 mL
2 tbsp	water	30 mL
1½ tsp	cider vinegar	7 mL
⅓ cup	chopped pecans, toasted (see tip, at left)	75 mL
	Caramel Frosting (page 82)	

1. In a large bowl, whisk together flour, brown sugar, cinnamon, baking soda, baking powder and salt. Set aside.

2. In a medium bowl, whisk together applesauce, oil, water and vinegar. Add to flour mixture and stir just until moistened. Gently stir in pecans.

3. If desired, place paper liners in wells. Fill each well with about 1½ tbsp (22 mL) batter. Bake for 6 to 8 minutes or until a tester inserted in the center of a cupcake comes out clean. Transfer cupcakes to a wire rack to cool. Repeat with the remaining batter.

4. Frost with Caramel Frosting.

Pink Lemonade Cupcakes

Roxanne's family spends many summer weekends at the Lake of the Ozarks, in Missouri. This recipe allows them to enjoy the taste of summer, as well as the memories, all year long.

Tips

For a more intense pink color, add a few drops of red food coloring to both the cake batter and the frosting.

Dilute any extra lemonade concentrate using the proportions recommended on the can, or to taste, and enjoy a glass while eating the cupcakes.

• Paper liners (optional)

2 cups	white cake mix	500 mL
1	egg, at room temperature	1
1	egg white, at room temperature	1
1/2 cup	frozen pink lemonade concentrate, thawed	125 mL
1/4 cup	vegetable oil	60 mL
	Pink Lemonade Frosting (page 86)	

1. In a large bowl, using an electric mixer on low speed, beat cake mix, egg, egg white, pink lemonade concentrate and oil for 30 seconds or until moistened. Beat on medium speed for 2 minutes.

2. If desired, place paper liners in wells. Fill each well with about 1 1/2 tbsp (22 mL) batter. Bake for 6 to 8 minutes or until a tester inserted in the center of a cupcake comes out clean. Transfer cupcakes to a wire rack to cool. Repeat with the remaining batter.

3. Frost with Pink Lemonade Frosting.

Cherry Limeade Cupcakes

**Makes
30 to 34 cupcakes**

We often drive to Wichita, Kansas, to tape television shows, and one treat of the day (besides best friends talking nonstop as we drive) is always an ice-cold limeade at a local drive-in. Nothing is as refreshing on a hot summer day as a cherry limeade, and we have captured the flavor of that drink in these cupcakes.

Tips

We know it takes a minute to freshly squeeze the juice from a lime, but the flavor of the cupcakes will be so much better — you will be glad you did. One lime will yield about 1½ tbsp (22 mL) juice and 1 tsp (5 mL) zest.

If desired, garnish each cupcake with ¼ of a very thin slice of lime and ½ maraschino cherry.

If a milder lime flavor is desired, reduce the lime juice to 2 tbsp (30 mL) and add 2 tbsp (30 mL) water.

- Paper liners (optional)

2 cups	white cake mix	500 mL
2	eggs, at room temperature	2
¾ cup	low-fat cherry yogurt	175 mL
	Grated zest of 1 lime	
¼ cup	freshly squeezed lime juice (see tip, at left)	60 mL
3 tbsp	vegetable oil	45 mL
3	drops red food coloring	3
¼ cup	finely chopped well-drained maraschino cherries	60 mL
	Cherry Lime Frosting (variation, page 81)	

1. In a large bowl, using an electric mixer on low speed, beat cake mix, eggs, yogurt, lime zest, lime juice, oil and food coloring for 30 seconds or until moistened. Beat on medium speed for 2 minutes. Gently stir in cherries.

2. If desired, place paper liners in wells. Fill each well with about 1½ tbsp (22 mL) batter. Bake for 6 to 8 minutes or until a tester inserted in the center of a cupcake comes out clean. Transfer cupcakes to a wire rack to cool. Repeat with the remaining batter.

3. Frost with Cherry Lime Frosting.

Chocolate Buttermilk Cupcakes (page 23) and
Coconut Cream Cupcakes (page 56)

Red Velvet Cupcakes (page 25)

Princess Pink Party Cupcakes (page 37)

Cookies and Cream Cupcakes (page 39)

Cherry Cupcakes (page 58)

Mojito Tart Cakes (page 64)

Pumpkin Cheesecakes with Caramel Pecan Topping (page 76)

Raspberry Streusel Muffins (page 106)

Summertime Herb Muffins (page 109)

Pineapple Cupcakes

• •

**Makes
26 to 28 cupcakes**

You'll dream of seaside
sunsets and tropical
getaways while baking
these pineapple tidbits.
You'd never guess
that these moist and
flavorful cupcakes
don't use oil or butter!

Tip

To enhance the tropical
flavor, add ¼ cup (60 mL)
toasted sweetened flaked
coconut with the pineapple.
Sprinkle frosted cupcakes
with additional toasted
coconut.

• Paper liners (optional)

1	can (8 oz/227 mL) crushed pineapple in its own juice	1
2 cups	yellow cake mix	500 mL
2	eggs, at room temperature	2
	Pineapple Buttercream Frosting (variation, page 80)	

1. Drain pineapple, reserving juice. Measure out and set aside 3 tbsp (45 mL) pineapple juice for use in the frosting.

2. In a large bowl, using an electric mixer on low speed, beat pineapple, the remaining pineapple juice, cake mix and eggs for 30 seconds or until moistened. Beat on medium speed for 2 minutes.

3. If desired, place paper liners in wells. Fill each well with about 1½ tbsp (22 mL) batter. Bake for 6 to 8 minutes or until a tester inserted in the center of a cupcake comes out clean. Transfer cupcakes to a wire rack to cool. Repeat with the remaining batter.

4. Prepare Pineapple Buttercream Frosting using the reserved pineapple juice. Spread over cupcakes.

Sugar and Spice Cupcakes

Do you like snickerdoodles? They are one of our favorite cookies, and they were the inspiration for these cupcakes.

Tip

Did you forget to set out the butter so that it will soften? Cut it into slices, place on a microwave-safe glass plate and microwave on Medium-Low (20%) for 10 to 15 seconds or until starting to soften. Let butter stand for about 10 minutes, then proceed with the recipe.

• Paper liners (optional)

Cupcakes

1½ cups	all-purpose flour	375 mL
1½ tsp	baking powder	7 mL
½ tsp	ground nutmeg	2 mL
¼ tsp	salt	1 mL
¾ cup	granulated sugar	175 mL
½ cup	butter, softened	125 mL
2	eggs, at room temperature	2
¾ cup	milk	175 mL
1 tsp	vanilla extract	5 mL

Filling and Topping

1½ tsp	granulated sugar	7 mL
½ tsp	ground cinnamon	2 mL
	Buttercream Frosting (page 80)	

1. *Cupcakes:* In a medium bowl, whisk together flour, baking powder, nutmeg and salt. Set aside.

2. In a large bowl, using an electric mixer on medium-high speed, beat sugar and butter for 1 to 2 minutes or until fluffy. Add eggs, one at a time, beating well after each addition. Add flour mixture alternately with milk, making three additions of flour and two of milk and beating until smooth. Beat in vanilla.

3. *Filling:* In a small bowl, combine sugar and cinnamon. Set half aside for garnish.

4. If desired, place paper liners in wells. Fill each well with about 1 tbsp (15 mL) batter. Using a total of about ¼ to ½ tsp (1 to 2 mL) cinnamon-sugar per batch of 8 cupcakes, very lightly sprinkle cinnamon-sugar over the batter in each well. Add 1½ tsp (7 mL) more batter to each well. Bake for 6 to 8 minutes or until a tester inserted in the center of a cupcake comes out clean. Transfer cupcakes to a wire rack to cool. Repeat with the remaining batter.

5. *Topping:* Frost with Buttercream Frosting. Using a fine-mesh sieve, sift the remaining cinnamon-sugar lightly over cupcakes.

Cupcakes Galore

Black Forest Cupcakes

Coffee makes a perfect accompaniment to these rich, dense chocolate cupcakes filled with moist, flavorful cherries and just a hint of Kirsch.

Tip

If desired, pipe or dollop a small amount of sweetened whipped cream on top of each frosted cupcake before adding the cherry. Here's how to make sweetened whipped cream: In a small bowl, using an electric mixer on high speed, beat ½ cup (125 mL) heavy or whipping (35%) cream until frothy. Add 1 tbsp (15 mL) confectioners' (icing) sugar and beat until stiff.

• Paper liners (optional)

½ cup	dried cherries, chopped	125 mL
2 tbsp	Kirsch or maraschino cherry juice	30 mL
2 cups	chocolate fudge cake mix	500 mL
2	eggs, at room temperature	2
½ cup	water	125 mL
¼ cup	vegetable oil	60 mL
	Chocolate Fudge Icing (page 92)	
17 to 19	maraschino cherries, drained and halved	17 to 19

1. In a small bowl, combine cherries and Kirsch. Let stand for 10 minutes.

2. In a large bowl, using an electric mixer on low speed, beat cake mix, cherry mixture, eggs, water and oil for 30 seconds or until moistened. Beat on medium speed for 2 minutes.

3. If desired, place paper liners in wells. Fill each well with about 1½ tbsp (22 mL) batter. Bake for 6 to 8 minutes or until a tester inserted in the center of a cupcake comes out clean. Transfer cupcakes to a wire rack to cool. Repeat with the remaining batter.

4. Spread with Chocolate Fudge Icing. Garnish each with half a maraschino cherry.

Caramel Pecan Chocolate Cupcakes

These delightful chocolate cupcakes, frosted with caramel and topped with a pecan half, will remind you of Turtles candies.

Tips

This is an easy, old-fashioned, one-bowl cake. While the mixing method is different from the traditional method, the results are still moist and flavorful. You will enjoy the great flavor — and the fact that you only have one bowl to wash.

No buttermilk on hand? Stir 1 1/4 tsp (6 mL) lemon juice or white vinegar into 1/3 cup (75 mL) milk. Let stand for 5 to 10 minutes or until thickened. Proceed with the recipe.

Toasting pecans intensifies their flavor. Spread pecan halves in a single layer on a baking sheet. Bake at 350°F (180°C) for 6 to 8 minutes or until lightly browned. Let cool.

- Paper liners (optional)

3/4 cup	all-purpose flour	175 mL
3/4 cup	granulated sugar	175 mL
6 tbsp	unsweetened cocoa powder	90 mL
1 tsp	baking soda	5 mL
1/2 tsp	baking powder	2 mL
1/4 tsp	salt	1 mL
1	egg, at room temperature	1
1/3 cup	buttermilk	75 mL
1/3 cup	warm water	75 mL
2 tbsp	vegetable oil	30 mL
1 tsp	vanilla extract	5 mL
	Caramel Frosting (page 82)	
	Chocolate Drizzle (page 92)	
24	pecan halves, toasted (see tip, at left)	24

1. In a large bowl, whisk together flour, sugar, cocoa, baking soda, baking powder and salt.

2. Add egg, buttermilk, water, oil and vanilla to flour mixture and, using an electric mixer on medium speed, beat until blended and smooth.

3. If desired, place paper liners in wells. Fill each well with about 1 1/2 tbsp (22 mL) batter. Bake for 6 to 8 minutes or until a tester inserted in the center of a cupcake comes out clean. Transfer cupcakes to a wire rack to cool. Repeat with the remaining batter.

4. Frost with Caramel Frosting, then drizzle with Chocolate Drizzle. Garnish each cupcake with a toasted pecan half.

Salted Caramel Cupcakes

Buttery, rich, salted caramel candies have long been a favorite in Brittany, a region of France. Today, that flavor is trendy and is incorporated into many desserts worldwide. Every time we taste these luscious cupcakes, we are reminded of our trip to France — a truly memorable excursion we shared with Roxanne's cookbook club.

Tip

Fleur de sel is a type of sea salt, harvested by hand in Brittany. Finding it may mean a trip to a specialty food store, but the wonderful flavor is worth the time and expense.

Variation

Salted Caramel Chocolate Cupcakes: Add a Chocolate Drizzle (page 92) over the Caramel Frosting, then sprinkle with fleur de sel. Or make your favorite chocolate cupcakes (Chocolate Cupcakes, page 22, and Chocolate Buttermilk Cupcakes, page 23, are both wonderful), then frost them with Caramel Frosting and sprinkle with fleur de sel.

• Paper liners (optional)

1½ cups	all-purpose flour	375 mL
2 tsp	baking powder	10 mL
¼ tsp	baking soda	1 mL
¼ tsp	salt	1 mL
¾ cup	packed brown sugar	175 mL
¼ cup	granulated sugar	60 mL
½ cup	butter, softened	125 mL
2	eggs, at room temperature	2
1 tsp	vanilla extract	5 mL
½ cup	milk	125 mL
	Caramel Frosting (page 82)	
	Fleur de sel	

1. In a medium bowl, whisk together flour, baking powder, baking soda and salt. Set aside.

2. In a large bowl, using an electric mixer on medium-high speed, beat brown sugar, granulated sugar and butter for 1 to 2 minutes or until fluffy. Add eggs, one at a time, beating well after each addition. Beat in vanilla. Add flour mixture alternately with milk, making three additions of flour and two of milk and beating on low speed until smooth.

3. If desired, place paper liners in wells. Fill each well with about 1½ tbsp (22 mL) batter. Bake for 6 to 8 minutes or until a tester inserted in the center of a cupcake comes out clean. Transfer cupcakes to a wire rack to cool. Repeat with the remaining batter.

4. Frost with Caramel Frosting. Lightly sprinkle each cupcake with fleur de sel.

Dulce de Leche Cupcakes

**Makes
30 to 32 cupcakes**

Dulce de leche — a
rich caramel popular
in Latin America — is
quickly becoming a
favorite worldwide.
If you aren't familiar
with dulce de leche,
these cupcakes will
introduce you to its
truly wonderful flavor!
Kathy's husband,
David, asks for these
again and again.

Tip

Dulce de leche is a thick,
sweet caramel and is now
readily available canned or
in jars. Look for it in larger
grocery stores, shelved with
the Latin American foods
or with the condensed milk.
One 14-oz (398 mL) can or
jar will provide plenty of
dulce de leche for both the
cake and the frosting.

- Paper liners (optional)

Cupcakes

1½ cups	all-purpose flour	375 mL
2 tsp	baking powder	10 mL
¼ tsp	baking soda	1 mL
¼ tsp	salt	1 mL
1 cup	dulce de leche	250 mL
½ cup	butter, softened	125 mL
⅓ cup	granulated sugar	75 mL
⅓ cup	packed brown sugar	75 mL
2	eggs, at room temperature	2
1 tsp	vanilla extract	5 mL
½ cup	milk	125 mL

Dulce de Leche Buttercream Frosting

½ cup	butter, softened	125 mL
3 tbsp	dulce de leche	45 mL
3 cups	confectioners' (icing) sugar	750 mL
3 to 4 tbsp	milk	45 mL to 60 mL
½ tsp	vanilla extract	2 mL

1. *Cupcakes:* In a medium bowl, whisk together flour, baking powder, baking soda and salt. Set aside.

2. In a large bowl, using an electric mixer on medium-high speed, beat dulce de leche and butter for 1 minute or until creamy. Beat in granulated sugar and brown sugar for 1 minute or until light and creamy. Add eggs, one at a time, beating well after each addition. Beat in vanilla. Add flour mixture alternately with milk, making three additions of flour and two of milk and beating on low speed until smooth.

3. If desired, place paper liners in wells. Fill each well with about 1½ tbsp (22 mL) batter. Bake for 6 to 8 minutes or until a tester inserted in the center of a cupcake comes out clean. Transfer cupcakes to a wire rack to cool. Repeat with the remaining batter.

4. *Frosting:* In a medium bowl, using an electric mixer on medium-high speed, beat butter and dulce de leche for 1 minute or until light and creamy. Reduce speed to medium and gradually beat in confectioners' sugar. Beat in 3 tbsp (45 mL) milk and vanilla. Beat in an additional 1 tbsp (15 mL) milk if a thinner frosting is desired. Frost cooled cupcakes.

Coconut Cream Cupcakes

• •

**Makes
36 to 40 cupcakes**

You don't need to
make a coconut
cream pie to enjoy
rich coconut flavor —
it is captured in these
moist cupcakes.

• •

Tips

Coconut milk is readily
available at most larger
grocery stores, often
shelved with the Asian
foods or canned milk. Do
not confuse coconut milk
with sweetened cream of
coconut, a canned product
often used for cocktails.
If coconut milk is not
available, substitute water
mixed with 1 tsp (5 mL)
coconut extract.

For Snowball Cupcakes,
sprinkle each frosted
cupcake generously with
untoasted sweetened
flaked coconut.

• Food processor
• Paper liners (optional)

2½ cups	sweetened flaked coconut, divided	625 mL
1	package (18.25 oz/515 g) white cake mix	1
1	can (14 oz/400 mL) coconut milk, divided	1
	Egg whites and oil as called for on cake mix package	
	Coconut Cream Frosting (page 85)	

1. In a food processor fitted with a metal blade, process ½ cup (125 mL) of the flaked coconut until very finely chopped (the texture of coarse meal).

2. In a large bowl, whisk together finely chopped coconut and cake mix. Substitute coconut milk for water as called for on cake mix package and add to coconut mixture. (Use the remaining coconut milk to make the frosting.) Add eggs whites and oil. Using an electric mixer on low speed, beat for 30 seconds or until moistened. Beat on medium speed for 2 minutes.

3. If desired, place paper liners in wells. Fill each well with about 1½ tbsp (22 mL) batter. Bake for 6 to 8 minutes or until a tester inserted in the center of a cupcake comes out clean. Transfer cupcakes to a wire rack to cool. Repeat with the remaining batter.

4. Meanwhile, preheat oven to 350°F (180°C). Spread the remaining flaked coconut in a thin, even layer on a baking sheet. Bake for about 5 minutes or until golden. Let cool.

5. Frost with Coconut Cream Frosting and sprinkle evenly with toasted coconut.

Dainty Lemon Cupcakes

· ·

**Makes
30 to 34 cupcakes**

Lemon curd adds a
delightful, intense
lemon flavor to these
cupcakes.

· ·

Tip

To easily frost these
cupcakes, use an icing bag
fitted with a large star tip
to pipe the frosting over
the lemon curd.

• Paper liners (optional)

2 cups	lemon cake mix	500 mL
2	eggs, at room temperature	2
⅔ cup	lemon curd, divided	150 mL
⅔ cup	water	150 mL
3 tbsp	vegetable oil	45 mL
	Lemon Buttercream Frosting (page 80)	

1. In a large bowl, using an electric mixer on low speed, beat cake mix, eggs, 3 tbsp (45 mL) of the lemon curd, water and oil for 30 seconds or until moistened. Beat on medium speed for 2 minutes.

2. If desired, place paper liners in wells. Fill each well with about 1½ tbsp (22 mL) batter. Bake for 6 to 8 minutes or until a tester inserted in the center of a cupcake comes out clean. Transfer cupcakes to a wire rack to cool. Repeat with the remaining batter.

3. Spread lemon curd over cupcakes. Dollop or pipe Lemon Buttercream Frosting over the lemon curd.

Cherry Cupcakes

Each of these dainty
morsels has a cherry
surprise inside!

Tips

For added sparkle, sprinkle
each frosted cupcake with
coarse red or pink sugar.

Although inserting a tester
into the center of each
cupcake is a standard way
to test for doneness, it
is not recommended for
these cupcakes, since they
are filled with cherries. To
test doneness, lightly and
carefully touch the top of
a cupcake. If done, it will
spring back.

Variation

Chocolate Cherry Cupcakes:
Prepare with chocolate
cake mix instead of white
cake mix.

• Paper liners (optional)

2 cups	white cake mix	500 mL
1	egg	1
1	egg white	1
10 tbsp	milk	150 mL
1/4 cup	vegetable oil	60 mL
1/2 tsp	almond extract	2 mL
30 to 34	maraschino cherries	30 to 34
	Cherry Buttercream Frosting (page 81)	

1. In a large bowl, using an electric mixer on low speed, beat cake mix, egg, egg white, milk, oil and almond extract for 30 seconds or until moistened. Beat on medium speed for 2 minutes.

2. If desired, place paper liners in wells. Fill each well with about $1\frac{1}{2}$ tbsp (22 mL) batter. Place a maraschino cherry in the center of each well. Bake for 6 to 8 minutes or until tops spring back when lightly touched. Transfer cupcakes to a wire rack to cool. Repeat with the remaining batter.

3. Frost with Cherry Buttercream Frosting.

Café au Lait Cupcakes

Makes 22 to 24 cupcakes

How about a café au lait cupcake with a cup of coffee? Or forget the coffee and just enjoy the cupcake.

Variation

Stir ¼ cup (60 mL) mini semisweet chocolate chips into the batter after the last addition of flour.

- Paper liners (optional)

1½ cups	all-purpose flour	375 mL
1½ tsp	baking powder	7 mL
¼ tsp	salt	1 mL
½ cup	granulated sugar	125 mL
⅓ cup	packed brown sugar	75 mL
⅓ cup	butter, softened	75 mL
2	eggs, at room temperature	2
⅔ cup	dairy French vanilla–flavored coffee creamer	150 mL
¼ cup	cold strong brewed coffee	60 mL
	Chocolate Coffee Icing (page 91)	

1. In a small bowl, whisk together flour, baking powder and salt. Set aside.

2. In a medium bowl, using an electric mixer on medium-high speed, beat granulated sugar, brown sugar and butter for 1 to 2 minutes or until fluffy. Add eggs, one at a time, beating well after each addition.

3. In another small bowl, combine coffee creamer and coffee.

4. Add flour mixture to sugar mixture alternately with coffee mixture, making three additions of flour and two of coffee and beating on low speed until smooth.

5. If desired, place paper liners in wells. Fill each well with about 1½ tbsp (22 mL) batter. Bake for 6 to 8 minutes or until a tester inserted in the center of a cupcake comes out clean. Transfer cupcakes to a wire rack to cool. Repeat with the remaining batter.

6. Spread with Chocolate Coffee Icing.

Kahlúa Cupcakes

**Makes
30 to 32 cupcakes**

Don't wait for Cinco de Mayo or another fiesta to enjoy these fabulous cupcakes — they are just too good!

Tips

This is an easy, old-fashioned, one-bowl cake. While the mixing method is different from the traditional method, the results are still moist and flavorful. You will enjoy the great flavor — and the fact that you only have one bowl to wash.

No buttermilk on hand? Stir 1½ tsp (7 mL) lemon juice or white vinegar into ½ cup (125 mL) milk. Let stand for 5 to 10 minutes or until thickened. Proceed with the recipe.

For a nonalcoholic version, substitute additional strong brewed coffee for the Kahlúa.

• Paper liners (optional)

1 cup	all-purpose flour	250 mL
½ cup	granulated sugar	125 mL
½ cup	packed brown sugar	125 mL
½ cup	unsweetened cocoa powder	125 mL
1 tsp	baking soda	5 mL
½ tsp	baking powder	2 mL
¼ tsp	salt	1 mL
1	egg	1
½ cup	buttermilk	125 mL
¼ cup	vegetable oil	60 mL
1 tsp	vanilla extract	5 mL
¼ cup	cold strong brewed coffee	60 mL
¼ cup	Kahlúa	60 mL
	Chocolate Kahlúa Icing (variation, page 91)	

1. In a large bowl, whisk together flour, granulated sugar, brown sugar, cocoa, baking soda, baking powder and salt.

2. Add egg, buttermilk, oil and vanilla to flour mixture and, using an electric mixer on medium speed, beat until blended and smooth. Using a wooden spoon, gently stir in coffee and Kahlúa until mixture is smooth.

3. If desired, place paper liners in wells. Fill each well with about 1½ tbsp (22 mL) batter. Bake for 6 to 8 minutes or until a tester inserted in the center of a cupcake comes out clean. Transfer cupcakes to a wire rack to cool. Repeat with the remaining batter.

4. Spread with Chocolate Kahlúa Icing.

Crème de Menthe Cupcakes

**Makes
30 to 34 cupcakes**

This is one of those times when you have to choose — start with a white cake mix or a chocolate cake mix? Either way, the Crème de Menthe Frosting and Chocolate Drizzle make these cupcakes truly awesome.

- Paper liners (optional)

2 cups	white cake mix or chocolate cake mix	500 mL
1	egg	1
1/2 cup	sour cream	125 mL
1/4 cup	water	60 mL
3 tbsp	vegetable oil	45 mL
1/4 cup	mini semisweet chocolate chips	60 mL
1/2 tsp	peppermint extract	2 mL
	Crème de Menthe Frosting (page 86)	
	Chocolate Drizzle (page 92)	

1. In a large bowl, using an electric mixer on low speed, beat cake mix, egg, sour cream, water and oil for 30 seconds or until moistened. Beat on medium speed for 2 minutes. Stir in chocolate chips and peppermint extract.

2. If desired, place paper liners in wells. Fill each well with about 1 1/2 tbsp (22 mL) batter. Bake for 6 to 8 minutes or until a tester inserted in the center of a cupcake comes out clean. Transfer cupcakes to a wire rack to cool. Repeat with the remaining batter.

3. Frost with Crème de Menthe Frosting, then drizzle with Chocolate Drizzle.

Island Rum Cakelets

These cupcakes, flavored with rum and orange juice, invite you to take a mini vacation to the tropical islands. Sit back and enjoy!

Tips

Did you forget to set out the butter so that it will soften? Cut it into slices, place on a microwave-safe glass plate and microwave on Medium-Low (20%) for 10 to 15 seconds or until starting to soften. Let butter stand for about 10 minutes, then proceed with the recipe.

A rasp grater, such as a Microplane, is the perfect tool for grating citrus zest. Wash the fruit and pat it dry, then grate it with the rasp using a light motion. For the best flavor, grate only the colored portion of the peel, avoiding the bitter white pith underneath. The fine side of a box cheese grater is a good alternative to a rasp.

- Paper liners (optional)

Cupcakes

1½ cups	all-purpose flour	375 mL
1½ tsp	baking powder	7 mL
½ tsp	baking soda	2 mL
½ tsp	ground nutmeg	2 mL
¼ tsp	salt	1 mL
1 cup	granulated sugar	250 mL
½ cup	butter, softened	125 mL
3	eggs, at room temperature	3
	Grated zest of 1 orange	
⅓ cup	freshly squeezed orange juice	75 mL
2 tbsp	rum (preferably golden)	30 mL

Glaze

2 tbsp	butter	30 mL
¼ cup	granulated sugar	60 mL
2 tbsp	freshly squeezed orange juice	30 mL
1 tbsp	rum (preferably golden)	15 mL
	Orange Rum Buttercream Frosting (variation, page 88)	

1. *Cupcakes:* In a medium bowl, whisk together flour, baking powder, baking soda, nutmeg and salt. Set aside.

2. In a large bowl, using an electric mixer on medium-high speed, beat sugar and butter for 1 to 2 minutes or until fluffy. Add eggs, one at a time, beating well after each addition. Beat in orange zest.

3. In a small bowl, combine orange juice and rum.

4. Add flour mixture to butter mixture alternately with juice mixture, making three additions of flour and two of juice and beating on low speed until smooth.

Tip

If you prefer, you can substitute 1 tsp (5 mL) rum extract and 5 tsp (25 mL) water for the rum in the cupcakes and $\frac{1}{2}$ tsp (2 mL) rum extract and 1 to 2 tsp (5 to 10 mL) more orange juice for the rum in the glaze.

5. If desired, place paper liners in wells. Fill each well with about $1\frac{1}{2}$ tbsp (22 mL) batter. Bake for 6 to 8 minutes or until a tester inserted in the center of a cupcake comes out clean. Transfer cupcakes to a wire rack to cool. Repeat with the remaining batter.

6. *Glaze:* Place butter in a microwave-safe glass bowl. Microwave on High for 30 seconds or until melted. Stir in sugar and microwave on High for 30 seconds or until mixture is bubbly and sugar is melted. Stir in juice and rum.

7. Brush warm glaze over tops of cupcakes. Once it has soaked in, brush cupcakes lightly with glaze again, using all of the glaze. Frost with Orange Rum Buttercream Frosting.

Mojito Tart Cakes

Care for a cocktail? The flavors of a mojito — lime, rum and mint — are captured in these cupcakes. A party awaits any time you serve these.

Tips

Lime curd is a thick, creamy mixture made from lime juice. Look for it in jars, often shelved near the jams and jellies at the grocery store. Freeze leftover lime curd in an airtight container for up to 1 year. Thaw curd overnight in the refrigerator and use within 4 weeks of thawing.

If desired, garnish with mint leaves and tiny curls of lime zest or lime wedges.

- Paper liners (optional)

1¾ cups	all-purpose flour	425 mL
1 tsp	baking powder	5 mL
½ tsp	baking soda	2 mL
¼ tsp	salt	1 mL
1 cup	granulated sugar	250 mL
½ cup	butter, softened	125 mL
2	eggs, at room temperature	2
⅓ cup	sour cream	75 mL
	Grated zest of 1 lime	
⅓ cup	milk	75 mL
2 tbsp	rum (preferably golden)	30 mL
2 tbsp	freshly squeezed lime juice	30 mL
1 tsp	peppermint extract	5 mL
¾ cup	lime curd	175 mL
	Mojito Rum Frosting (page 88)	

1. In a small bowl, whisk together flour, baking powder, baking soda and salt. Set aside.

2. In a large bowl, using an electric mixer on medium-high speed, beat sugar and butter for 1 to 2 minutes or until fluffy. Add eggs, one at a time, beating well after each addition. Beat in sour cream and lime zest. Reduce mixer speed to low and beat in one-third of the flour mixture. Beat in milk, then another third of the flour mixture, then rum and lime juice. Beat in the remaining flour mixture. Stir in peppermint extract.

3. If desired, place paper liners in wells. Fill each well with about 1½ tbsp (22 mL) batter. Bake for 6 to 8 minutes or until a tester inserted in the center of a cupcake comes out clean. Transfer cupcakes to a wire rack to cool. Repeat with the remaining batter.

4. Spread lime curd over cupcakes, then frost with Mojito Rum Frosting.

Mini Cheesecakes

Chocolate Truffle Cheesecakes

Truffle — a rich, chocolate confection — is the perfect name for these gorgeous cheesecakes. Although they last just a couple of bites, the intense chocolate flavor shines in each one.

Tips

Do not let cheesecakes stand at room temperature for more than 2 hours. Always store cheesecakes, sweet or savory, in the refrigerator. When entertaining, set out just those that will be eaten soon, and replenish with chilled cheesecakes as needed.

Use a small offset spatula to lift the cheesecakes from the wells. Be careful not to scrape the coating on the cupcake maker.

- Food processor
- Paper liners

Crusts

6	cream-filled chocolate sandwich cookies	6
1 tbsp	butter, melted	15 mL

Filling

2 oz	semisweet chocolate, chopped	60 g
8 oz	cream cheese, softened	250 g
1/4 cup	granulated sugar	60 mL
1 tbsp	all-purpose flour	15 mL
1	egg, at room temperature	1
1 tbsp	heavy or whipping (35%) cream	15 mL
1/2 tsp	vanilla extract	2 mL

Topping

1/4 cup	chopped semisweet chocolate or semisweet chocolate chips (about 1 1/2 oz/45 g)	60 mL
2 tbsp	heavy or whipping (35%) cream	30 mL
1/4 tsp	vanilla extract	1 mL

1. *Crusts:* In a food processor fitted with a metal blade, process cookies to fine, even crumbs. Add butter and pulse to blend.

2. Place a paper liner in each well. Spoon about 1 1/2 tsp (7 mL) crumb mixture into the bottom of each liner. Use the pie forming tool to tap crust into liner.

3. *Filling:* Place chocolate in a small microwave-safe glass bowl. Microwave on High in 30-second intervals, stirring after each, until melted.

4. In a medium bowl, using an electric mixer on medium speed, beat cream cheese for 1 minute or until fluffy. Beat in sugar and flour until smooth. Reduce mixer speed to low and beat in egg, cream and vanilla just until smooth (do not overbeat). Beat in melted chocolate.

Tips

For ease of decorating, spoon topping into a food storage bag and snip off a corner. Drizzle topping in fine, thin lines over the top of each cheesecake.

For a showstopper, melt 1 oz (30 g) white chocolate and drizzle over each cheesecake after the semisweet chocolate topping. The contrasting color is beautiful.

5. Spoon about 1 1/2 tbsp (22 mL) filling over crust in each liner. Bake for 7 to 9 minutes or until filling is puffed at the edges and softly set at the center. Using a small offset spatula, carefully transfer cheesecakes to a wire rack to cool. Repeat with the remaining crusts and filling.

6. *Topping:* In a small microwave-safe glass bowl, combine chocolate and cream. Microwave on High for 30 seconds or until cream comes to a boil. Stir until chocolate is melted and mixture is smooth. Stir in vanilla. Drizzle about 1 tsp (5 mL) topping on each cheesecake. Refrigerate for at least 3 hours, until chilled and set, or for up to 5 days.

German Chocolate Cheesecakes

The classic Coconut
Pecan Frosting makes
a wonderful partner for
these little cheesecake
gems.

Tips

Do not let cheesecakes
stand at room temperature
for more than 2 hours.
Always store cheesecakes,
sweet or savory, in the
refrigerator. When
entertaining, set out just
those that will be eaten
soon, and replenish with
chilled cheesecakes as
needed.

Use a small offset spatula
to lift the cheesecakes from
the wells. Be careful not to
scrape the coating on the
cupcake maker.

- Food processor
- Paper liners

Crusts

6	cream-filled chocolate sandwich cookies	6
1 tbsp	butter, melted	15 mL

Filling

2 oz	sweet chocolate (such as Baker's German's or Baker's) or semisweet chocolate, chopped	60 g
8 oz	cream cheese, softened	250 g
1/3 cup	granulated sugar	75 mL
1 tbsp	all-purpose flour	15 mL
1	egg, at room temperature	1
1/2 tsp	vanilla extract	2 mL

Topping

Coconut Pecan Frosting (page 85)

1. *Crusts:* In a food processor fitted with a metal blade, process cookies to fine, even crumbs. Add butter and pulse to blend.

2. Place a paper liner in each well. Spoon about 1 1/2 tsp (7 mL) crumb mixture into the bottom of each liner. Use the pie forming tool to tap crust into liner.

3. *Filling:* Place chocolate in a small microwave-safe glass bowl. Microwave on High in 30-second intervals, stirring after each, until melted.

4. In a medium bowl, using an electric mixer on medium speed, beat cream cheese for 1 minute or until fluffy. Beat in sugar and flour until smooth. Reduce mixer speed to low and beat in egg and vanilla just until smooth (do not overbeat). Beat in melted chocolate.

5. Spoon about 1 1/2 tbsp (22 mL) filling over crust in each liner. Bake for 7 to 9 minutes or until filling is puffed at the edges and softly set at the center. Using a small offset spatula, carefully transfer cheesecakes to a wire rack to cool. Repeat with the remaining crusts and filling. Refrigerate for at least 3 hours, until chilled and set, or for up to 5 days.

6. *Topping:* Frost each cheesecake with about 1 1/2 tbsp (22 mL) frosting.

Eggnog Cheesecakes

Makes 14 to 16 cheesecakes

Each Christmas, Roxanne, her husband, Bob Bateman, and their daughter, Grace, share an eggnog toast. Then they use the leftover eggnog (or maybe we should call it the "planned-over eggnog") to make these holiday favorites.

Tips

Believe it or not, Roxanne's family often requests these in the summer, when eggnog is not available. You can substitute heavy or whipping (35%) cream mixed with $\frac{1}{2}$ tsp (2 mL) vanilla extract and an extra pinch of ground nutmeg.

You can substitute rum extract or vanilla extract for the brandy extract.

• Paper liners

Crusts

$\frac{1}{2}$ cup	graham wafer crumbs (see tip, page 70)	125 mL
1 tbsp	granulated sugar	15 mL
2 tbsp	butter, melted	30 mL

Filling

8 oz	cream cheese, softened	250 g
$\frac{1}{4}$ cup	granulated sugar	60 mL
1 tbsp	all-purpose flour	15 mL
1	egg, at room temperature	1
Pinch	ground nutmeg	Pinch
$\frac{1}{4}$ cup	eggnog (see tip, at left)	60 mL
$\frac{1}{4}$ tsp	brandy extract (see tip, at left)	1 mL

Topping

7 to 8	candied cherries, cut in half	7 to 8

1. *Crusts:* In a small bowl, combine graham wafer crumbs and sugar. Stir in butter.

2. Place a paper liner in each well. Spoon about $1\frac{1}{2}$ tsp (7 mL) crumb mixture into the bottom of each liner. Use the pie forming tool to tap crust into liner.

3. *Filling:* In a medium bowl, using an electric mixer on medium speed, beat cream cheese for 1 minute or until fluffy. Beat in sugar and flour until smooth. Reduce mixer speed to low and beat in egg until just combined. Beat in nutmeg, eggnog and brandy extract just until smooth (do not overbeat).

4. Spoon about $1\frac{1}{2}$ tbsp (22 mL) filling over crust in each liner. Bake for 7 to 9 minutes or until filling is puffed at the edges and softly set at the center. Using a small offset spatula, carefully transfer cheesecakes to a wire rack to cool. Repeat with the remaining crusts and filling.

5. *Topping:* Place a candied cherry half, cut side down, in the center of each cheesecake. Refrigerate for at least 3 hours, until chilled and set, or for up to 5 days.

Praline Cheesecakes

• •

Makes 16 to 18 cheesecakes

We both enjoy traveling to New Orleans and have been lucky enough to explore the city while attending professional food conventions. This recipe brings back memories of the many good times we've shared in the Crescent City.

....

Tips

Graham wafer crumbs can be purchased ready-made, but if you can't find them, you'll need about two 4$\frac{3}{4}$- by 2$\frac{1}{4}$-inch (11.5 by 5.5 cm) wafers to make $\frac{1}{2}$ cup (125 mL).

Do not let cheesecakes stand at room temperature for more than 2 hours. Always store cheesecakes, sweet or savory, in the refrigerator. When entertaining, set out just those that will be eaten soon, and replenish with chilled cheesecakes as needed.

Toasting pecans intensifies their flavor. Spread chopped pecans in a single layer on a baking sheet. Bake at 350°F (180°C) for 5 to 7 minutes or until lightly browned. Let cool, then measure.

• Paper liners

Crusts

$\frac{1}{2}$ cup	graham wafer crumbs (see tip, at left)	125 mL
1 tbsp	granulated sugar	15 mL
2 tbsp	butter, melted	30 mL

Filling

8 oz	cream cheese, softened	250 g
$\frac{1}{2}$ cup	granulated sugar	125 mL
1 tbsp	all-purpose flour	15 mL
2	eggs, at room temperature	2
1 tsp	vanilla extract	5 mL
$\frac{1}{4}$ cup	chopped pecans, toasted (see tip, at left)	60 mL

Topping

1 tbsp	packed brown sugar	15 mL
1 tbsp	cornstarch	15 mL
$\frac{1}{2}$ cup	dark (golden) corn syrup	125 mL
1 tsp	vanilla extract	5 mL
$\frac{1}{2}$ cup	chopped pecans, toasted	125 mL

1. *Crusts:* In a small bowl, combine graham wafer crumbs and sugar. Stir in butter.

2. Place a paper liner in each well. Spoon about 1$\frac{1}{2}$ tsp (7 mL) crumb mixture into the bottom of each liner. Use the pie forming tool to tap crust into liner.

3. *Filling:* In a medium bowl, using an electric mixer on medium speed, beat cream cheese for 1 minute or until fluffy. Beat in sugar and flour until smooth. Reduce mixer speed to low and beat in eggs and vanilla just until smooth (do not overbeat). Stir in pecans.

Tips

Use a small offset spatula to lift the cheesecakes from the wells. Be careful not to scrape the coating on the cupcake maker.

Topping will thicken if left to cool. To use it, place in a microwave-safe glass bowl and microwave on High in 30-second intervals until spoonable.

Variation

Omit the topping. Instead, stir the 1/2 cup (125 mL) pecans into 1/2 cup (125 mL) caramel ice cream topping or sundae syrup and serve on cheesecakes.

4. Spoon about 1 1/2 tbsp (22 mL) filling over crust in each liner. Bake for 7 to 9 minutes or until filling is puffed at the edges and softly set at the center. Using a small offset spatula, carefully transfer cheesecakes to a wire rack to cool. Repeat with the remaining crusts and filling. Refrigerate for at least 3 hours, until chilled and set, or for up to 5 days.

5. *Topping:* Just before serving, in a small saucepan, combine brown sugar, cornstarch, corn syrup and vanilla. Cook over medium heat, stirring constantly, for 2 to 3 minutes or until bubbling and thick. Stir in pecans. Drizzle over cheesecakes.

Ginger Cheesecakes

Makes 14
to 16 cheesecakes

The ginger flavor is mild but captivating in these mini cheesecakes, and the ginger-spiked whipped cream makes the perfect topping.

Tips

Use a food processor fitted with a metal blade to quickly make fine crumbs from the cookies. You'll need about ten 2-inch (5 cm) gingersnap cookies to make $\frac{1}{2}$ cup (125 mL) crumbs.

For a stronger ginger flavor, add 2 tsp (10 mL) finely chopped crystallized ginger to the filling with the sugar.

- Paper liners

Crusts

$\frac{1}{2}$ cup	gingersnap cookie crumbs (see tip, at left)	125 mL
2 tbsp	butter, melted	30 mL

Filling

8 oz	cream cheese, softened	250 g
$\frac{1}{2}$ cup	granulated sugar	125 mL
1	egg, at room temperature	1
$\frac{1}{2}$ tsp	ground ginger	2 mL
1 tsp	freshly squeezed lemon juice	5 mL

Topping

$\frac{1}{2}$ cup	heavy or whipping (35%) cream	125 mL
1 tbsp	confectioners' (icing) sugar	15 mL
$\frac{1}{4}$ tsp	ground ginger	1 mL

1. *Crusts:* In a small bowl, combine cookie crumbs and butter. Stir well.

2. Place a paper liner in each well. Spoon about $1\frac{1}{2}$ tsp (7 mL) crumb mixture into the bottom of each liner. Use the pie forming tool to tap crust into liner.

3. *Filling:* In a medium bowl, using an electric mixer on medium speed, beat cream cheese for 1 minute or until fluffy. Beat in sugar until smooth. Reduce mixer speed to low and beat in egg until just combined. Beat in ginger and lemon juice just until smooth (do not overbeat).

4. Spoon about $1\frac{1}{2}$ tbsp (22 mL) filling over crust in each liner. Bake for 7 to 9 minutes or until filling is puffed at the edges and softly set at the center. Using a small offset spatula, carefully transfer cheesecakes to a wire rack to cool. Repeat with the remaining crusts and filling. Refrigerate for at least 3 hours, until chilled and set, or for up to 5 days.

5. *Topping:* Just before serving, in a small bowl, using an electric mixer on high speed, beat cream until frothy. Beat in confectioners' sugar and ginger until stiff peaks form. Dollop or pipe onto each cheesecake.

Refreshing Lemon Cheesecakes

Makes 14 to 16 cheesecakes

Is there any flavor more refreshing than lemon? The tartness of the citrus combined with the richness of the cream cheese is captivating in these mini cheesecakes.

Tips
If desired, spoon about 1 tsp (5 mL) lemon curd onto each cheesecake.

Garnish the top of each cheesecake with fresh raspberries or blueberries, if desired.

Variation
Omit the graham wafer crumb mixture and instead place a whole vanilla wafer in each paper liner; proceed with the recipe.

- Paper liners

Crusts

½ cup	graham wafer crumbs (see tip, page 70)	125 mL
1 tbsp	granulated sugar	15 mL
¼ tsp	ground cinnamon	1 mL
2 tbsp	butter, melted	30 mL

Filling

8 oz	cream cheese, softened	250 g
⅓ cup	granulated sugar	75 mL
	Grated zest of 1 lemon	
1	egg, at room temperature	1
2 tbsp	freshly squeezed lemon juice	30 mL
½ tsp	vanilla extract	2 mL

1. *Crusts:* In a small bowl, combine graham wafer crumbs, sugar and cinnamon. Stir in butter.

2. Place a paper liner in each well. Spoon about 1½ tsp (7 mL) crumb mixture into the bottom of each liner. Use the pie forming tool to tap crust into liner.

3. *Filling:* In a medium bowl, using an electric mixer on medium speed, beat cream cheese for 1 minute or until fluffy. Beat in sugar and lemon zest until smooth. Reduce mixer speed to low and beat in egg until just combined. Beat in lemon juice and vanilla just until smooth (do not overbeat).

4. Spoon about 1½ tbsp (22 mL) filling over crust in each liner. Bake for 7 to 9 minutes or until filling is puffed at the edges and softly set at the center. Using a small offset spatula, carefully transfer cheesecakes to a wire rack to cool. Repeat with the remaining crusts and filling. Refrigerate for at least 3 hours, until chilled and set, or for up to 5 days.

Cherry Cheesecakes

Makes 14 to 16 cheesecakes

The classic combination of cheesecakes and cherries always tastes wonderful, and the beautiful contrast in colors makes these mini treats welcome on any dessert buffet.

Tips

You can replace the cherry preserves with the cherry filling from Old-Fashioned Cherry Hand Pies (page 125) or canned cherry pie filling.

Use a small offset spatula to lift the cheesecakes from the wells. Be careful not to scrape the coating on the cupcake maker.

• Paper liners

Crusts

½ cup	graham wafer crumbs (see tip, page 76)	125 mL
1 tbsp	granulated sugar	15 mL
2 tbsp	butter, melted	30 mL

Filling

8 oz	cream cheese, softened	250 g
⅓ cup	granulated sugar	75 mL
1	egg, at room temperature	1
¼ tsp	almond extract	1 mL

Topping

⅓ cup	cherry preserves	75 mL

1. *Crusts:* In a small bowl, combine graham wafer crumbs and sugar. Stir in butter.

2. Place a paper liner in each well. Spoon about 1½ tsp (7 mL) crumb mixture into the bottom of each liner. Use the pie forming tool to tap crust into liner.

3. *Filling:* In a medium bowl, using an electric mixer on medium speed, beat cream cheese for 1 minute or until fluffy. Beat in sugar until smooth. Reduce mixer speed to low and beat in egg and almond extract just until smooth (do not overbeat).

4. Spoon about 1½ tbsp (22 mL) filling over crust in each liner. Bake for 7 to 9 minutes or until filling is puffed at the edges and softly set at the center. Using a small offset spatula, carefully transfer cheesecakes to a wire rack to cool. Repeat with the remaining crusts and filling. Refrigerate for at least 3 hours, until chilled and set, or for up to 5 days.

5. *Topping:* Just before serving, spoon cherry preserves onto each cheesecake.

Blueberry Cheesecakes

Makes 14 to 16 cheesecakes

These cheesecakes capture the essence of summer. Try pairing them with Cherry Cheesecakes (page 74) and Refreshing Lemon Cheesecakes (page 73) for a delicious assortment to serve at a get-together.

Tips

Use a food processor fitted with a metal blade to quickly make fine crumbs from the cookies. You'll need about six 2-inch (5 cm) diameter pecan shortbread cookies to make 1/2 cup (125 mL) crumbs.

Substitute blueberry preserves or blueberry pie filling for the fresh blueberry topping.

• Paper liners

Crusts

1/2 cup	pecan shortbread cookie crumbs (see tip, at left)	125 mL
1 tbsp	granulated sugar	15 mL
1 tbsp	butter, melted	15 mL

Filling

8 oz	cream cheese, softened	250 g
1/3 cup	granulated sugar	75 mL
1	egg, at room temperature	1
1/2 tsp	lemon extract	2 mL

Topping

1 tbsp	granulated sugar	15 mL
1 1/2 tsp	cornstarch	7 mL
3/4 cup	fresh or frozen blueberries	175 mL
1 1/2 tsp	freshly squeezed lemon juice	7 mL

1. *Crusts:* In a small bowl, combine cookie crumbs and sugar. Stir in butter.

2. Place a paper liner in each well. Spoon about 1 1/2 tsp (7 mL) crumb mixture into the bottom of each liner. Use the pie forming tool to tap crust into liner.

3. *Filling:* In a medium bowl, using an electric mixer on medium speed, beat cream cheese for 1 minute or until fluffy. Beat in sugar until smooth. Reduce mixer speed to low and beat in egg and lemon extract just until smooth (do not overbeat).

4. Spoon about 1 1/2 tbsp (22 mL) filling over crust in each liner. Bake for 7 to 9 minutes or until filling is puffed at the edges and softly set at the center. Using a small offset spatula, carefully transfer cheesecakes to a wire rack to cool. Repeat with the remaining crusts and filling. Refrigerate for at least 3 hours, until chilled and set, or for up to 5 days.

5. *Topping:* In a small saucepan, combine sugar and cornstarch. Stir in blueberries and lemon juice. Cook over low heat, stirring frequently, for 5 minutes or until berries are coated, sugar is dissolved and juices are slightly thickened. Remove from heat and let cool. Just before serving, spoon topping onto each cheesecake.

Pumpkin Cheesecakes with Caramel Pecan Topping

Makes 16 to 18 cheesecakes

Pumpkin, spices and pecans make a winning combination. In fact, with this much flavor, you'll want to make these often.

Tips

Graham wafer crumbs can be purchased ready-made, but if you can't find them, you'll need about two 4¾- by 2¼-inch (11.5 by 5.5 cm) wafers to make ½ cup (125 mL).

Toasting pecans intensifies their flavor. Spread chopped pecans in a single layer on a baking sheet. Bake at 350°F (180°C) for 5 to 7 minutes or until lightly browned. Let cool, then measure.

- Paper liners

Crusts

½ cup	graham wafer crumbs (see tip, at left)	125 mL
1 tbsp	granulated sugar	15 mL
¼ tsp	ground cinnamon	1 mL
2 tbsp	butter, melted	30 mL

Filling

8 oz	cream cheese, softened	250 g
¼ cup	granulated sugar	60 mL
2 tbsp	packed brown sugar	30 mL
1	egg, at room temperature	1
⅓ cup	canned pumpkin purée (not pie filling)	75 mL
1 tbsp	all-purpose flour	15 mL
¼ tsp	ground cinnamon	1 mL
1 tbsp	heavy or whipping (35%) cream	15 mL

Topping

1 tbsp	butter	15 mL
¼ cup	packed brown sugar	60 mL
2 tbsp	heavy or whipping (35%) cream	30 mL
⅓ cup	chopped pecans, toasted (see tip, at left)	75 mL
½ tsp	vanilla extract	2 mL

1. *Crusts:* In a small bowl, combine graham wafer crumbs, sugar and cinnamon. Stir in butter.

2. Place a paper liner in each well. Spoon about 1½ tsp (7 mL) crumb mixture into the bottom of each liner. Use the pie forming tool to tap crust into liner.

3. *Filling:* In a medium bowl, using an electric mixer on medium speed, beat cream cheese for 1 minute or until fluffy. Beat in granulated sugar and brown sugar until smooth. Reduce mixer speed to low and beat in egg and pumpkin until just combined. Beat in flour, cinnamon and cream just until smooth (do not overbeat).

Tips

Do not let cheesecakes stand at room temperature for more than 2 hours. Always store cheesecakes, sweet or savory, in the refrigerator. When entertaining, set out just those that will be eaten soon, and replenish with chilled cheesecakes as needed.

Use a small offset spatula to lift the cheesecakes from the wells. Be careful not to scrape the coating on the cupcake maker.

4. Spoon about $1\frac{1}{2}$ tbsp (22 mL) filling over crust in each liner. Bake for 7 to 9 minutes or until filling is puffed at the edges and softly set at the center. Using a small offset spatula, carefully transfer cheesecakes to a wire rack to cool. Repeat with the remaining crusts and filling. Refrigerate for at least 3 hours, until chilled and set.

5. *Topping:* Place butter in a small microwave-safe glass bowl. Microwave on High for 30 to 40 seconds or until melted. Stir in brown sugar and microwave on High for 30 seconds. Stir well. Microwave in 10-second intervals, stirring after each, until sugar is dissolved and mixture is bubbling. Stir in cream until well blended. Microwave on High in 10-second intervals until mixture is bubbling. Stir until smooth. Stir in pecans and vanilla. Let cool for 3 minutes, then spoon topping over each cheesecake. Serve immediately or refrigerate for up to 5 days.

Southwest Appetizer Cheesecakes

Kathy's family has served a Southwest cheesecake appetizer for many years. Now, that same savory, cheesy flavor is captured in these mini cheesecakes, perfect for an appetizer buffet.

Tips

Use a food processor fitted with a metal blade to crush the chips. You'll need about 3 cups (750 mL) whole tortilla chips to make ¾ cup (175 mL) finely crushed chips.

For an especially attractive presentation, garnish the cheesecakes with a variety of colorful toppings, such as salsa, sliced pitted ripe olives, sliced jalapeño peppers, fresh cilantro leaves and/or sour cream.

• Paper liners

Crusts

¾ cup	finely crushed tortilla chips (see tip, at left)	175 mL
2 tbsp	butter, melted	30 mL

Filling

8 oz	cream cheese, softened	250 g
1 cup	shredded Cheddar, Colby-Jack or Monterey Jack cheese	250 mL
½ cup	sour cream	125 mL
1	egg, at room temperature	1
1 tbsp	all-purpose flour	15 mL
½ tsp	ground cumin	2 mL
¼ tsp	garlic powder	1 mL
3 tbsp	heavy or whipping (35%) cream	45 mL
¼ tsp	hot pepper sauce	1 mL

1. *Crusts:* In a small bowl, combine crushed tortilla chips and butter.

2. Place a paper liner in each well. Spoon about 1½ tsp (7 mL) crumb mixture into the bottom of each liner. Use the pie forming tool to tap crust into liner.

3. *Filling:* In a large bowl, using an electric mixer on medium speed, beat cream cheese for 1 minute or until fluffy. Beat in Cheddar and sour cream. Reduce mixer speed to low and beat in egg just until combined. Beat in flour, cumin, garlic powder, cream and hot pepper sauce until well blended.

4. Spoon about 1½ tbsp (22 mL) filling over crust in each liner. Bake for 7 to 9 minutes or until filling is puffed at the edges and softly set at the center. Using a small offset spatula, carefully transfer cheesecakes to a wire rack to cool. Repeat with the remaining crusts and filling. Refrigerate for at least 3 hours, until chilled and set, or for up to 5 days.

Frostings and Glazes

Buttercream Frosting

This popular frosting is perfect for almost any cupcake. It is creamy and rich, yet it is so easy to make.

Tip

You can tint frosting to any color by adding drops of liquid food coloring. For a more intense color, use gel or paste food colors.

½ cup	butter, softened	125 mL
3 cups	confectioners' (icing) sugar	750 mL
3 to 4 tbsp	milk	45 to 60 mL
½ tsp	vanilla extract	2 mL

1. In a medium bowl, using an electric mixer on medium-high speed, beat butter for 1 minute or until light and creamy. Gradually beat in sugar until blended. Beat in 3 tbsp (45 mL) milk and vanilla until light and fluffy.

2. If a thinner frosting is desired, beat in an additional 1 tbsp (15 mL) milk.

Lemon Buttercream Frosting

Use this inviting, fresh-tasting frosting on Lemon Cupcakes (page 27), of course, but it is also really good on Gingerbread Cupcakes (page 32) and Yellow Cupcakes (page 20).

Tip

If you want the frosting to be a brighter yellow, tint it with 1 or 2 drops of yellow food coloring.

½ cup	butter, softened	125 mL
3 cups	confectioners' (icing) sugar	750 mL
3 to 4 tbsp	freshly squeezed lemon juice	45 to 60 mL

1. In a medium bowl, using an electric mixer on medium-high speed, beat butter for 1 minute or until light and creamy. Gradually beat in sugar until blended. Beat in 3 tbsp (45 mL) lemon juice until light and fluffy.

2. If a thinner frosting is desired, beat in an additional 1 tbsp (15 mL) lemon juice.

Variation

Pineapple Buttercream Frosting: Substitute pineapple juice for the lemon juice. This recipe is perfect with Pineapple Cupcakes (page 49).

Orange Blossom Buttercream Frosting

Makes about 1¾ cups (425 mL)

The refreshing orange flavor makes this the ideal frosting to use on Orange Blossom Cupcakes (page 28), but try it on yellow cupcakes, vanilla cupcakes or chocolate cupcakes, too.

½ cup	butter, softened	125 mL
3 cups	confectioners' (icing) sugar	750 mL
3 to 4 tbsp	orange juice	45 to 60 mL
¼ tsp	orange extract	1 mL
2	drops red food coloring	2
2	drops yellow food coloring	2

1. In a medium bowl, using an electric mixer on medium-high speed, beat butter for 1 minute or until light and creamy. Gradually beat in sugar until blended. Beat in 3 tbsp (45 mL) orange juice, orange extract, red food coloring and yellow food coloring until light and fluffy.

2. If a thinner frosting is desired, beat in an additional 1 tbsp (15 mL) orange juice.

Cherry Buttercream Frosting

Makes about 1¾ cups (425 mL)

This frosting is perfect for Cherry Cupcakes (page 58), but it also complements any chocolate or vanilla cupcake.

½ cup	butter, softened	125 mL
3 cups	confectioners' (icing) sugar	750 mL
3 to 4 tbsp	maraschino cherry juice	45 to 60 mL
½ tsp	almond extract	2 mL

1. In a medium bowl, using an electric mixer on medium-high speed, beat butter for 1 minute or until light and creamy. Gradually beat in sugar until blended. Beat in 3 tbsp (45 mL) cherry juice and almond extract until light and fluffy.

2. If a thinner frosting is desired, beat in an additional 1 tbsp (15 mL) cherry juice.

Variation

Cherry Lime Frosting: Substitute 1 tsp (5 mL) freshly squeezed lime juice for the almond extract. Use to frost Cherry Limeade Cupcakes (page 48) or any vanilla or yellow cupcake.

Creamy Chocolate Frosting

Makes about 2 cups (500 mL)

This rich, creamy chocolate frosting will become a family favorite.

Variation

For a nutty flavor, add ¼ tsp (1 mL) almond extract with the corn syrup.

1 cup	semisweet chocolate chips	250 mL
½ cup	butter, softened	125 mL
2 cups	confectioners' (icing) sugar	500 mL
2 tsp	light (white or golden) corn syrup	10 mL
1 to 2 tbsp	milk	15 to 30 mL

1. Place chocolate chips in a small microwave-safe glass bowl. Microwave on High for 1 minute. Stir. Microwave on High in 30-second intervals, stirring after each, until melted. Let cool.

2. In a medium bowl, using an electric mixer on medium-high speed, beat butter for 1 minute or until light and creamy. Gradually beat in sugar until blended. Beat in corn syrup and melted chocolate. Beat in 1 tbsp (15 mL) milk until light and fluffy.

3. If a thinner frosting is desired, beat in an additional 1 tbsp (15 mL) milk.

Caramel Frosting

Makes about 1½ cups (375 mL)

You will find countless uses for this caramel frosting. You'll love it on Chocolate Cupcakes (page 22) and Applesauce Cupcakes (page 46), but don't stop there! Try it on Butter Pecan Cupcakes (page 30) and Banana Cupcakes (page 174) too.

¼ cup	butter, softened	60 mL
¼ cup	shortening	60 mL
3 tbsp	caramel ice cream topping or sundae syrup	45 mL
1 tsp	vanilla extract	5 mL
Pinch	salt	Pinch
2½ cups	confectioners' (icing) sugar	625 mL
1 tbsp	milk (optional)	15 mL

1. In a medium bowl, using an electric mixer on medium-high speed, beat butter and shortening for 1 minute or until light and creamy. Beat in caramel ice cream topping, vanilla and salt. Gradually beat in sugar until blended.

2. If a thinner frosting is desired, beat in milk.

Praline Frosting

You will think of a praline candy, straight from Louisiana, when you taste cupcakes topped with this brown sugar and pecan frosting. It is perfect on Butter Pecan Cupcakes (page 30), but it is also wonderful on Salted Caramel Cupcakes (page 54) and Applesauce Cupcakes (page 46).

Tips

Be sure to beat the frosting for at least 2 minutes before deciding whether additional confectioners' (icing) sugar is needed; this frosting thickens as it cools. If it gets too thick, thin it by beating in a little additional cream. It is best to make the frosting just before you intend to frost the cupcakes.

Store leftover frosting in an airtight container in the refrigerator for up to 2 weeks. Let warm to room temperature before using.

1⅓ cups	packed light brown sugar	325 mL
½ cup	whipping (35%) cream	125 mL
6 tbsp	butter	90 mL
2½ to 3 cups	confectioners' (icing) sugar	625 to 750 mL
1 tsp	vanilla extract	5 mL
1 cup	chopped pecans, toasted (see tip, page 76)	250 mL

1. In a small saucepan, combine brown sugar, cream and butter. Heat over medium heat, stirring occasionally, until butter is melted and mixture begins to boil. Boil for 1 minute, stirring occasionally. Pour into a medium bowl and let cool for 1 minute.

2. Using an electric mixer on high speed, gradually beat 2½ cups (625 mL) confectioners' sugar into brown sugar mixture until blended. Continue beating for 2 to 3 minutes or until smooth. Beat in vanilla.

3. If frosting is too thin, beat in more confectioners' sugar, 1 tbsp (15 mL) at a time, until frosting is desired consistency.

4. Frost cupcakes, then garnish with pecans.

Marshmallow Frosting

There are endless ways to enhance Babycakes with this creamy frosting. Roxanne's daughter, Grace, says it tastes like the marshmallow filling inside a chocolate-covered Easter bunny.

Tip

Store leftover frosting in an airtight container in the refrigerator for up to 2 weeks. Let warm to room temperature before using.

½ cup	butter, softened	125 mL
½ cup	marshmallow creme	125 mL
1 tsp	vanilla extract	5 mL
4½ cups	confectioners' (icing) sugar	1.125 L
4 to 5 tbsp	milk	60 to 75 mL

1. In a large bowl, using an electric mixer on medium-high speed, beat butter for 1 minute or until light and creamy. Beat in marshmallow creme and vanilla. Gradually beat in sugar until blended. Beat in 4 tbsp (60 mL) milk until creamy.

2. If a thinner frosting is desired, beat in an additional 1 tbsp (15 mL) milk.

Variation

Marshmallow Graham Frosting: Fold in 3 tbsp (45 mL) graham wafer crumbs when preparing this frosting for S'more Cupcakes (page 44).

Strawberry Frosting

Makes about 1⅔ cups (400 mL)

Thanks to frozen strawberries, this frosting can brag of a jewel-tone pink color and a fruity flavor.

Tip

If you want the frosting to be a brighter red, tint it with red food coloring.

¼ cup	butter, softened	60 mL
¼ cup	frozen halved strawberries in syrup, thawed	60 mL
2½ cups	confectioners' (icing) sugar	625 mL
1 to 2 tbsp	milk	15 to 30 mL

1. In a medium bowl, using an electric mixer on medium-high speed, beat butter for 1 minute or until fluffy. Beat in strawberries until well combined. Gradually beat in sugar until blended. Beat in 1 tbsp (15 mL) milk until light and fluffy.

2. If a thinner frosting is desired, beat in an additional 1 tbsp (15 mL) milk.

Coconut Cream Frosting

Makes about 1½ cups (375 mL)

This is the perfect frosting to use on Coconut Cream Cupcakes (page 56).

Tip

No coconut milk? Substitute milk and add ½ tsp (2 mL) coconut extract with the vanilla.

½ cup	butter, softened	125 mL
2½ cups	confectioners' (icing) sugar	625 mL
3 to 5 tbsp	coconut milk	45 to 75 mL
1 tsp	vanilla extract	5 mL

1. In a medium bowl, using an electric mixer on medium-high speed, beat butter for 1 minute or until light and creamy. Gradually beat in sugar until blended. Beat in 3 tbsp (45 mL) coconut milk and vanilla until light and fluffy.

2. If a thinner frosting is desired, beat in more coconut milk, 1 tbsp (15 mL) at a time, until frosting is desired consistency.

Coconut Pecan Frosting

Makes 1½ cups (375 mL)

This old-time favorite is a must for German Chocolate Cupcakes (page 24) and German Chocolate Cheesecakes (page 68).

Tip

Many people prefer the intensified flavors of toasted coconut and pecans in their frosting. To toast, spread coconut and chopped pecans in a single layer on a baking sheet. Bake at 350°F (180°C) for 5 to 7 minutes or until lightly browned. Let cool, then measure.

¾ cup	granulated sugar	175 mL
2	egg yolks	2
6 tbsp	butter	90 mL
⅓ cup	evaporated milk	75 mL
1 tsp	vanilla extract	5 mL
1⅓ cups	sweetened flaked coconut (see tip, at left)	325 mL
¾ cup	chopped pecans	175 mL

1. In a medium saucepan, combine sugar, egg yolks, butter, evaporated milk and vanilla. Cook over medium heat, stirring constantly, for 10 to 12 minutes or until thick and golden. Remove from heat and stir in coconut and pecans. Let cool for 20 minutes.

Pink Lemonade Frosting

Makes about 1¾ cups (425 mL)

Summertime flavors are captured in this frosting that's perfect for Pink Lemonade Cupcakes (page 47). It also adds refreshing zip to your other favorite cupcakes.

½ cup	butter, softened	125 mL
3 cups	confectioners' (icing) sugar	750 mL
3 to 4 tbsp	frozen pink lemonade concentrate, thawed	45 to 60 mL

1. In a medium bowl, using an electric mixer on medium-high speed, beat butter for 1 minute or until light and creamy. Gradually beat in sugar until blended. Beat in 3 tbsp (45 mL) pink lemonade concentrate until light and fluffy.

2. If a thinner frosting is desired, beat in an additional 1 tbsp (15 mL) pink lemonade concentrate.

Crème de Menthe Frosting

Makes about 1¾ cups (425 mL)

Frost Crème de Menthe Cupcakes (page 61) with this minty green frosting. And don't forget to prepare it when baking for St. Patrick's Day or Christmas!

Tip

For a nonalcoholic version, substitute milk or half-and-half (10%) cream for the crème de menthe and peppermint extract for the vanilla. Tint to the desired color with green food coloring.

½ cup	butter, softened	125 mL
3 cups	confectioners' (icing) sugar	750 mL
3 to 4 tbsp	green crème de menthe	45 to 60 mL
½ tsp	vanilla extract	2 mL

1. In a medium bowl, using an electric mixer on medium-high speed, beat butter for 1 minute or until light and creamy. Gradually beat in sugar until blended. Beat in 3 tbsp (45 mL) crème de menthe and vanilla until light and fluffy.

2. If a thinner frosting is desired, beat in an additional 1 tbsp (15 mL) crème de menthe.

Champagne Frosting

Makes about 1 cup (250 mL)

This frosting tastes great with Champagne Cupcakes (page 196), but it turns any cupcake into a celebration. Sprinkle frosted cupcakes with coarse white decorating sugar for a fun, festive look.

Tips

If you like to pipe the frosting on fairly thick, you may wish to double this recipe when pairing it with Champagne Cupcakes (page 196) so you will have plenty.

If desired, use Champagne flavoring, available from cake decorating stores, instead of Champagne, adding just a few drops or to taste. Add an additional 1 tbsp (15 mL) milk.

Store leftover frosting in an airtight container in the refrigerator for up to 2 weeks. Let warm to room temperature before using.

$1/3$ cup	butter, softened	75 mL
2 cups	confectioners' (icing) sugar	500 mL
1 to 2 tbsp	milk	15 to 30 mL
1 tbsp	Champagne or sparkling wine	15 mL
$1/2$ tsp	vanilla extract	2 mL
3 to 4	drops red food coloring	3 to 4

1. In a medium bowl, using an electric mixer on medium-high speed, beat butter for 1 minute or until light and creamy. Gradually beat in sugar until blended. Beat in 1 tbsp (15 mL) milk, Champagne, vanilla and food coloring until creamy.

2. If a thinner frosting is desired, beat in an additional 1 tbsp (15 mL) milk.

Mojito Rum Frosting

Makes about 1¾ cups (425 mL)

The mojito — that rum, lime and mint Cuban cocktail — inspires both the Mojito Tart Cakes (page 64) and this frosting.

Tips

For a nonalcoholic version, substitute ½ tsp (2 mL) rum extract for the rum.

Store leftover frosting in an airtight container in the refrigerator for up to 2 weeks. Let warm to room temperature before using.

Variation

Orange Rum Buttercream Frosting: Substitute freshly squeezed orange juice for the milk and vanilla for the peppermint extract.

½ cup	butter, softened	125 mL
3 cups	confectioners' (icing) sugar	750 mL
3 to 4 tbsp	milk	45 to 60 mL
1 tsp	rum (preferably golden)	5 mL
½ tsp	peppermint extract	2 mL

1. In a medium bowl, using an electric mixer on medium-high speed, beat butter for 1 minute or until light and creamy. Gradually beat in sugar until blended. Beat in 3 tbsp (45 mL) milk, rum and peppermint extract until light and fluffy.

2. If a thinner frosting is desired, beat in an additional 1 tbsp (15 mL) milk.

Decorator Frosting

Makes about 2½ cups (625 mL)

When you want to pipe frosting and you want a professional look, this is the frosting of choice. Since it is made with shortening instead of butter, it doesn't melt quite as easily as buttercream, so it is easier to use when piping more intricate designs.

Tips

For a truer white color, use colorless vanilla extract.

You can tint frosting to any color by adding drops of liquid food coloring. For a more intense color, use gel or paste food colors.

Store leftover frosting in an airtight container in the refrigerator for up to 2 weeks. Let warm to room temperature before using.

4 cups	confectioners' (icing) sugar	1 L
1 cup	shortening	250 mL
4 to 5 tbsp	milk	60 to 75 mL
1½ tsp	vanilla extract	7 mL

1. In a large bowl, using an electric mixer on low speed, beat sugar, shortening, 4 tbsp (60 mL) milk and vanilla until just blended. Beat on high speed for 3 to 5 minutes or until very light and fluffy.

2. If a thinner frosting is desired, beat in an additional 1 tbsp (15 mL) milk.

Cream Cheese Frosting

**Makes
about 1½ cups
(375 mL)**

This classic frosting
is super-creamy!

Tip

Store leftover frosting in
an airtight container in
the refrigerator for up to
5 days. Let warm to room
temperature before using.

3 oz	cream cheese, softened	90 g
¼ cup	butter, softened	60 mL
2¼ cups	confectioners' (icing) sugar	550 mL
½ tsp	vanilla extract	2 mL

1. In a medium bowl, using an electric mixer on
medium-high speed, beat cream cheese and butter
for 1 minute or until light and creamy. Gradually beat
in sugar until blended. Beat in vanilla.

Variation

Peppermint Cream Cheese Frosting: Substitute peppermint
extract for the vanilla.

Peanut Butter Cream Cheese Frosting

**Makes
about 1¾ cups
(425 mL)**

This frosting is fantastic
on Chocolate Peanut
Butter Cupcakes
(page 42), but it may
become such a favorite
that you'll use it on
any vanilla, yellow or
chocolate cupcake.

Tip

Store leftover frosting in
an airtight container in
the refrigerator for up to
5 days. Let warm to room
temperature before using.

3 oz	cream cheese, softened	90 g
¼ cup	butter, softened	60 mL
3 tbsp	creamy peanut butter	45 mL
2¼ cups	confectioners' (icing) sugar	550 mL
½ tsp	vanilla extract	2 mL

1. In a medium bowl, using an electric mixer on
medium-high speed, beat cream cheese, butter and
peanut butter for 1 minute or until light and creamy.
Gradually beat in sugar until blended. Beat in vanilla.

White Chocolate Cream Cheese Frosting

Makes about 1¾ cups (425 mL)

This elegant, luscious frosting is wonderful on White Chocolate Snowmen Cupcakes (page 206), but it can be used on any cupcake.

Tips

To melt white chocolate, place chopped white chocolate in a small microwave-safe glass bowl and microwave on High in 30-second intervals, stirring after each, until melted.

3 oz	cream cheese, softened	90 g
2 oz	white chocolate, melted (see tip, at left)	60 g
¼ cup	butter, softened	60 mL
2¼ cups	confectioners' (icing) sugar	550 mL
½ tsp	vanilla extract	2 mL

1. In a medium bowl, using an electric mixer on medium-high speed, beat cream cheese, white chocolate and butter for 1 minute or until light and creamy. Gradually beat in sugar until blended. Beat in vanilla.

Chocolate Coffee Icing

Makes about 1 cup (250 mL)

Our good friend and fellow cookbook author Karen Adler shared her mom's icing recipe with us, and we are so glad she did. It is terrific! Thanks, Karen.

Variation

Chocolate Kahlúa Icing: Replace half the coffee with 1½ tbsp (22 mL) Kahlúa.

6 tbsp	unsalted butter, softened	90 mL
2 cups	confectioners' (icing) sugar	500 mL
¼ cup	unsweetened cocoa powder	60 mL
3 tbsp	cold strong brewed coffee	45 mL
1 tsp	vanilla extract	5 mL
Pinch	salt	Pinch

1. In a medium bowl, using an electric mixer on high speed, beat butter for 1 minute or until light and creamy. Gradually beat in sugar until blended. Beat in cocoa, coffee, vanilla and salt until blended.

Chocolate Fudge Icing

Makes about 2 cups (500 mL)

This decadent topping will bring to mind a cross between chocolate frosting and hot fudge sauce. It's guaranteed to make any dessert a winner!

Tip

Store cocoa powder in an airtight container in a cool, dry place for up to 2 years.

1/3 cup	butter	75 mL
10 tbsp	unsweetened cocoa powder	150 mL
4 cups	confectioners' (icing) sugar	1 L
4 to 5 tbsp	milk	60 to 75 mL
1 tsp	vanilla extract	5 mL
1 tsp	light (white or golden) corn syrup	5 mL

1. In a small saucepan, melt butter over medium heat. Add cocoa, stirring constantly until mixture comes to a boil and is smooth. Pour into a medium bowl and let cool slightly.

2. Using an electric mixer on medium-high speed, gradually beat sugar into cocoa mixture until blended. Beat in 4 tbsp (60 mL) milk, vanilla and corn syrup until blended.

3. If a thinner icing is desired, beat in an additional 1 tbsp (15 mL) milk.

Chocolate Drizzle

Makes about 1/3 cup (75 mL)

This drizzle is especially good when spooned over a frosting, for that little "something extra."

Tip

For easy drizzling, fill a sealable food storage bag with Chocolate Drizzle, then snip off the corner.

1/3 cup	semisweet chocolate chips	75 mL
1 tbsp	milk	15 mL
1 tsp	light (white or golden) corn syrup	5 mL

1. In a small microwave-safe glass bowl, combine chocolate chips, milk and corn syrup. Microwave on High for 30 seconds. Stir until blended and thick. Let cool to lukewarm.

Vanilla Glaze

1 cup	confectioners' (icing) sugar	250 mL
1½ to	milk	22 to
2 tbsp		30 mL
½ tsp	vanilla extract	2 mL

Makes about ½ cup (125 mL)

Drizzle this simple glaze over any flavor of cupcake or muffin for a quick yet sweet finish.

Tip

For easy drizzling, fill a sealable food storage bag with Vanilla Glaze, then snip off the corner.

1. In a small bowl, whisk together sugar, 1½ tbsp (22 mL) milk and vanilla.

2. If a thinner glaze is desired, whisk in more milk, 1 tsp (5 mL) at a time.

Lemon Glaze

¾ cup	confectioners' (icing) sugar	175 mL
1½ to	freshly squeezed lemon juice	22 to
2 tbsp		30 mL

Makes about ⅓ cup (75 mL)

This light glaze makes an ideal topping for both cupcakes and muffins.

Tips

For added lemon flavor, blend in the grated zest of 1 lemon.

For easy drizzling, fill a sealable food storage bag with Lemon Glaze, then snip off the corner.

Variation

Orange Glaze: Substitute freshly squeezed orange juice for the lemon juice.

1. In a small bowl, whisk together sugar and 1 tbsp (15 mL) lemon juice.

2. If a thinner glaze is desired, whisk in more lemon juice, 1 tsp (5 mL) at a time.

Part 2

Muffins, Pies and Tarts

Muffins

Buttermilk Spice Tea Room Muffins

These muffins
are excellent at
breakfast or as an
accompaniment to a
luncheon salad. And
they taste great the
next day, too.

Tips

No buttermilk on hand?
Stir 1½ tsp (7 mL) white
vinegar or lemon juice into
6 tbsp (90 mL) milk. Let
stand for 5 to 10 minutes
or until thickened. Proceed
with the recipe.

Store leftover muffins in an
airtight container and plan
to serve within a day or two.
Or store in the freezer for
up to 3 months.

Variation

Stir ¼ cup (60 mL) cinnamon
chips or butterscotch chips
into the batter, if desired.

- Paper liners (optional)

Muffins

1¼ cups	all-purpose flour	300 mL
1 tsp	baking soda	5 mL
½ tsp	ground nutmeg	2 mL
½ tsp	ground cinnamon	2 mL
½ cup	granulated sugar	125 mL
½ cup	butter, softened	125 mL
1	egg	1
1	egg yolk	1
6 tbsp	buttermilk	90 mL

Topping

⅓ cup	chopped pecans	75 mL
¼ cup	granulated sugar	60 mL
¼ tsp	ground nutmeg	1 mL
¼ tsp	ground cinnamon	1 mL

1. *Muffins:* In a small bowl, whisk together flour, baking soda, nutmeg and cinnamon. Set aside.

2. In a medium bowl, using an electric mixer on medium speed, beat sugar and butter for 1 to 2 minutes or until fluffy. Add egg and egg yolk and beat for 1 minute. Add flour mixture alternately with buttermilk, making three additions of flour and two of buttermilk and beating until just blended.

3. *Topping:* In a small bowl, combine pecans, sugar, nutmeg and cinnamon.

4. If desired, place paper liners in wells. Fill each well with about 1½ tbsp (22 mL) batter. Sprinkle about 1 tsp (5 mL) topping over the batter in each well. Bake for 6 to 8 minutes or until a tester inserted in the center of a muffin comes out clean. Transfer muffins to a wire rack to cool. Repeat with the remaining batter and topping.

Spicy Bran Muffins

Just the perfect hint of cinnamon, ginger and nutmeg flavors these bran muffins. They taste too good to be good for you.

Tips

Do not substitute a nugget, stick or cluster-type bran cereal, such as Bran Buds or All-Bran, for the raisin bran flakes cereal in this recipe. These cereals absorb liquid quite differently from the flakes and won't produce the same results.

Store leftover muffins in an airtight container and plan to serve within a day or two. Or store in the freezer for up to 3 months.

• Paper liners (optional)

2 cups	raisin bran flakes cereal	500 mL
⅔ cup	milk	150 mL
⅔ cup	all-purpose flour	150 mL
⅓ cup	granulated sugar	75 mL
2 tsp	baking powder	10 mL
½ tsp	pumpkin pie spice	2 mL
¼ tsp	salt	1 mL
1	egg, lightly beaten	1
3 tbsp	vegetable oil	45 mL

1. In a large bowl, combine cereal and milk. Let stand for 2 minutes.

2. In another large bowl, whisk together flour, sugar, baking powder, pumpkin pie spice and salt. Set aside.

3. Stir egg and oil into cereal mixture. Stir into flour mixture until just blended.

4. If desired, place paper liners in wells. Fill each well with about 1½ tbsp (22 mL) batter. Bake for 6 to 8 minutes or until a tester inserted in the center of a muffin comes out clean. Transfer muffins to a wire rack to cool. Repeat with the remaining batter.

Honey Nut Muffins

**Makes
14 to 16 muffins**

These muffins are made with both honey and sugar, yet the sweetness is mild and elusive. You will love serving them with jam for breakfast, or with a salad for lunch or dinner.

Tips

Toasting pecans intensifies their flavor. Spread chopped pecans in a single layer on a baking sheet. Bake at 350°F (180°C) for 5 to 7 minutes or until lightly browned. Let cool, then measure.

These muffins are especially good with Honey Butter (page 16).

• Paper liners (optional)

1 cup	all-purpose flour	250 mL
3 tbsp	granulated sugar	45 mL
1½ tsp	baking powder	7 mL
¼ tsp	ground nutmeg	1 mL
Pinch	salt	Pinch
1	egg	1
½ cup	milk	125 mL
2 tbsp	liquid honey	30 mL
2 tbsp	butter, melted	30 mL
¼ cup	chopped pecans, toasted (see tip, at left)	60 mL

1. In a large bowl, whisk together flour, sugar, baking powder, nutmeg and salt. Set aside.

2. In a medium bowl, whisk egg until blended. Whisk in milk, honey and butter. Stir into flour mixture until just blended. Gently stir in pecans.

3. If desired, place paper liners in wells. Fill each well with about 1½ tbsp (22 mL) batter. Bake for 5 to 7 minutes or until a tester inserted in the center of a muffin comes out clean. Transfer muffins to a wire rack to cool. Repeat with the remaining batter.

Almond Poppy Seed Muffins

There's no need to stop at a coffee shop or bakery to buy muffins on your way to work. Now you can quickly make a batch of these and share them with everyone at the office.

Tip

If desired, drizzle Vanilla Glaze (page 93) over these muffins.

• Paper liners (optional)

1/3 cup	milk	75 mL
1	egg	1
1/2 tsp	vanilla extract	2 mL
1/2 tsp	almond extract	2 mL
1/3 cup	vegetable oil	75 mL
3/4 cup	all-purpose flour	175 mL
10 tbsp	granulated sugar	150 mL
1/2 tsp	baking powder	2 mL
1/4 tsp	salt	1 mL
1 tsp	poppy seeds	5 mL

1. In a medium bowl, combine, in this order, milk, egg, vanilla, almond extract, oil, flour, sugar, baking powder and salt. Using an electric mixer on medium speed, beat for 2 minutes. Using a wooden spoon, stir in poppy seeds.

2. If desired, place paper liners in wells. Fill each well with about $1^1/_2$ tbsp (22 mL) batter. Bake for 5 to 7 minutes or until a tester inserted in the center of a muffin comes out clean. Transfer muffins to a wire rack to cool. Repeat with the remaining batter.

Lemon Poppy Seed Muffins

**Makes
26 to 28 muffins**

Baking mix makes
these muffins easy
and quick, without
sacrificing that
homemade goodness.

Tips

When measuring baking
mix, be sure to spoon it
into the measuring cup and
level it off (do not scoop
the baking mix up with the
measuring cup).

One lemon will yield about
3 tbsp (45 mL) juice and
2 to 3 tsp (10 to 15 mL) zest.
You'll get the maximum
amount of juice if it's at
room temperature. Rolling
the lemon firmly across the
counter a couple of times
before juicing it will also
increase the amount of juice
you get.

These muffins are best
served warm or on the
day they are baked. If you
store leftovers for another
day, be sure to keep them
refrigerated in an airtight
container.

• Paper liners (optional)

Muffins

1/3 cup	granulated sugar	75 mL
	Grated zest of 1 lemon	
2	eggs	2
1/4 cup	freshly squeezed lemon juice	60 mL
1/4 cup	water	60 mL
2 tbsp	vegetable oil	30 mL
2 cups	baking mix, such as Bisquick	500 mL
1 tbsp	poppy seeds	15 mL

Glaze

1/4 cup	confectioners' (icing) sugar	60 mL
1 tsp	grated lemon zest	5 mL
2 tsp	freshly squeezed lemon juice	10 mL
2 tbsp	coarse white sanding sugar crystals or decorating sugar (optional)	30 mL

1. *Muffins:* In a large bowl, whisk together sugar, lemon zest, eggs, lemon juice, water and oil until blended. Stir in baking mix and poppy seeds until just blended.

2. If desired, place paper liners in wells. Fill each well with about $1\frac{1}{2}$ tbsp (22 mL) batter. Bake for 6 to 8 minutes or until a tester inserted in the center of a muffin comes out clean. Transfer muffins to a wire rack to cool. Repeat with the remaining batter.

3. *Glaze:* Whisk together confectioners' sugar, lemon zest and lemon juice. Drizzle glaze over muffins. Immediately sprinkle lightly with sugar crystals (if using).

Lemon-Glazed Muffins

Add a little sunshine to your morning. These are so easy, you can make them even on busy days.

Tips

Zest only the colored portion of the peel, avoiding the bitter white pith underneath.

Muffins taste best freshly baked, and with Babycakes that couldn't be easier or faster! These tiny muffins are about two bites, but since they are so tasty, it is hard to eat just one. If you're making muffins for a group or to serve as refreshments, make plenty.

Store leftover muffins in an airtight container and plan to serve within a day or two. Or store in the freezer for up to 3 months.

• Paper liners (optional)

1 1/2 cups	all-purpose flour	375 mL
1/3 cup	granulated sugar	75 mL
2 tsp	baking powder	10 mL
1/4 tsp	salt	1 mL
1	egg	1
1/2 cup	milk	125 mL
1/4 cup	vegetable oil	60 mL
	Grated zest of 1 lemon	
	Lemon Glaze (page 93)	

1. In a large bowl, whisk together flour, sugar, baking powder and salt. Set aside.

2. In a medium bowl, whisk together egg, milk, oil and lemon zest until blended. Stir into flour mixture until just blended.

3. If desired, place paper liners in wells. Fill each well with about 1 1/2 tbsp (22 mL) batter. Bake for 5 to 7 minutes or until a tester inserted in the center of a muffin comes out clean. Transfer muffins to a wire rack to cool. Repeat with the remaining batter.

4. Drizzle Lemon Glaze over muffins.

Orange Streusel Muffins

These make sweet treats for breakfast, brunch or anytime. Try serving them with Citrus Butter (page 16).

Tips

For ease, zest the orange first, then juice it. One orange will yield about ⅓ cup (75 mL) juice and 1½ tbsp (22 mL) zest. Zest only the colored portion of the peel, avoiding the bitter white pith underneath.

When measuring out the marmalade, try to avoid any large pieces of peel.

• Paper liners (optional)

Muffins

1½ cups	all-purpose flour	375 mL
¼ cup	granulated sugar	60 mL
1½ tsp	baking powder	7 mL
¼ tsp	salt	1 mL
1	egg	1
	Grated zest of 1 orange	
⅓ cup	freshly squeezed orange juice	75 mL
¼ cup	milk	60 mL
3 tbsp	vegetable oil	45 mL
2 tbsp	orange marmalade	30 mL

Streusel

4 tsp	granulated sugar	20 mL
1 tbsp	all-purpose flour	15 mL
½ tsp	ground cinnamon	2 mL
1 tbsp	butter, softened	15 mL

1. *Muffins:* In a large bowl, whisk together flour, sugar, baking powder and salt. Set aside.

2. In a small bowl, whisk together egg, orange zest, orange juice, milk, oil and marmalade until blended. Stir into flour mixture until just blended.

3. *Streusel:* In a small bowl, combine sugar, flour and cinnamon. Using a pastry blender or your fingers, cut in butter until crumbly and well combined.

4. If desired, place paper liners in wells. Fill each well with about 1½ tbsp (22 mL) batter. Sprinkle about ½ tsp (2 mL) streusel over the batter in each well. Bake for 5 to 7 minutes or until a tester inserted in the center of a muffin comes out clean. Transfer muffins to a wire rack to cool. Repeat with the remaining batter and streusel.

Banana Nut Muffins

**Makes
26 to 28 muffins**

Banana nut muffins
are so moist and
wonderful, it's no
wonder they're an
all-time classic!

Tips

Be sure to use ripe bananas
in this recipe, as they have
more flavor.

When bananas become
overripe, place them in the
refrigerator for up to 3 days.
While the peels will turn
dark, the fruit will be fine.
For longer storage, they
can be frozen. Simply place
the unpeeled bananas in a
sealable food storage bag,
label and freeze. The peel
will become quite dark. To
use, thaw overnight in the
refrigerator. While the fruit
will be soft, it is perfect to
use in banana bread or in
these muffins.

Store leftover muffins in an
airtight container and plan
to serve within a day or two.
Or store in the freezer for
up to 3 months.

• Paper liners (optional)		
1 1/2 cups	all-purpose flour	375 mL
1 tsp	baking soda	5 mL
1/2 tsp	ground cinnamon	2 mL
1/4 tsp	salt	1 mL
1 1/2 cups	mashed ripe banana (about 3 medium)	375 mL
1/2 tsp	freshly squeezed lemon juice	2 mL
1/3 cup	butter, melted	75 mL
1/2 cup	granulated sugar	125 mL
1/4 cup	packed brown sugar	60 mL
1	egg	1
1/2 tsp	vanilla extract	2 mL
1/2 cup	chopped pecans or walnuts, toasted (see tip, page 104)	125 mL

1. In a small bowl, whisk together flour, baking soda, cinnamon and salt. Set aside.

2. In a large bowl, combine banana and lemon juice until well blended. Stir in butter. Whisk in granulated sugar, brown sugar, egg and vanilla until well blended. Stir in flour mixture until just blended. Gently stir in pecans.

3. If desired, place paper liners in wells. Fill each well with about 1 1/2 tbsp (22 mL) batter. Bake for 6 to 8 minutes or until a tester inserted in the center of a muffin comes out clean. Transfer muffins to a wire rack to cool. Repeat with the remaining batter.

Apple Harvest Muffins

**Makes
22 to 24 muffins**

Apple season in the Midwest means trips to the orchard. We both grew up near a popular local orchard, and although we didn't know each other as children, we both went with our parents to that orchard to pick fruit. What memories! The orchard had a fantastic restaurant that featured all kinds of apple treats — including their famous apple cider and apple butter — and these muffins are inspired by those wonderful flavors.

Tips

Toasting pecans intensifies their flavor. Spread chopped pecans in a single layer on a baking sheet. Bake at 350°F (180°C) for 5 to 7 minutes or until lightly browned. Let cool, then measure.

Store leftover muffins in an airtight container and plan to serve within a day or two. Or store in the freezer for up to 3 months.

• Paper liners (optional)

Muffins

1¾ cups	all-purpose flour	425 mL
¼ cup	granulated sugar	60 mL
2 tbsp	packed brown sugar	30 mL
2 tsp	baking powder	10 mL
1 tsp	pumpkin pie spice	5 mL
¼ tsp	salt	1 mL
1	egg	1
½ cup	milk	125 mL
½ cup	apple butter	125 mL
¼ cup	unsweetened apple cider or apple juice	60 mL
¼ cup	vegetable oil	60 mL
¼ cup	chopped pecans, toasted (see tip, below)	60 mL

Glaze

2 tsp	granulated sugar	10 mL
1 cup	unsweetened apple cider	250 mL

1. *Muffins:* In a large bowl, whisk together flour, granulated sugar, brown sugar, baking powder, pumpkin pie spice and salt. Set aside.

2. In a medium bowl, whisk together egg, milk, apple butter, apple cider and oil. Stir into flour mixture until just blended. Gently stir in pecans.

3. If desired, place paper liners in wells. Fill each well with about 1½ tbsp (22 mL) batter. Bake for 5 to 7 minutes or until a tester inserted in the center of a muffin comes out clean. Transfer muffins to a wire rack to cool. Repeat with the remaining batter.

4. *Glaze:* In a small saucepan, combine sugar and cider; bring to a boil over medium heat. Boil for about 15 minutes or until cider is reduced by about half and is syrupy. Brush some of the syrup lightly over each muffin; let syrup soak in, then brush again with the remaining syrup.

Blueberry Muffins

Makes 14 to 16 muffins

Blueberries just never go out of style. Perhaps it's because they are a nutritional powerhouse and shine like jewels in warm, freshly baked muffins.

Tips

Select smaller blueberries for these muffins and save larger berries for other uses.

Frozen blueberries can be used instead of fresh. There's no need to thaw them before stirring them into the batter.

If desired, drizzle Vanilla Glaze (page 93) over these muffins.

• Paper liners (optional)

¾ cup	small blueberries	175 mL
1 cup + 2 tbsp	all-purpose flour, divided	280 mL
1½ tsp	baking powder	7 mL
½ tsp	ground cinnamon	2 mL
¼ tsp	salt	1 mL
¼ cup	granulated sugar	60 mL
¼ cup	butter, softened	60 mL
1	egg	1
½ cup	milk	125 mL

1. In a small bowl, combine blueberries and 2 tbsp (30 mL) of the flour. Toss gently to coat. Set aside.

2. In another small bowl, whisk together the remaining flour, baking powder, cinnamon and salt. Set aside.

3. In a large bowl, using an electric mixer on medium speed, beat sugar and butter for 1 to 2 minutes or until fluffy. Add egg and beat for 1 minute. Beat in milk. Stir in flour mixture until just blended. Gently stir in blueberry mixture.

4. If desired, place paper liners in wells. Fill each well with about 1½ tbsp (22 mL) batter. Bake for 6 to 8 minutes or until a tester inserted in the center of a muffin comes out clean. Transfer muffins to a wire rack to cool. Repeat with the remaining batter.

Raspberry Streusel Muffins

● ●

**Makes
22 to 24 muffins**

Roxanne's friend Sue Monaghan shared this recipe with us, and we are so appreciative! Prepare these using either fresh or frozen raspberries. They are a nice change of pace from blueberry.

● ● ● ● ● ● ● ● ● ● ● ● ● ● ● ● ● ● ●

Tips

Fresh raspberries freeze very well. Wash them gently so that they maintain their delicate shape, then pat dry with a paper towel. Arrange them in a single layer on a baking sheet and place in the freezer. Once frozen, transfer the berries to a freezer bag, seal and date the bag. Return them to the freezer, where they will keep for up to 1 year.

There's no need to thaw frozen raspberries before stirring them into the batter.

Store leftover muffins in an airtight container and plan to serve within a day or two. Or store in the freezer for up to 3 months.

● **Paper liners (optional)**

Muffins

1½ cups	all-purpose flour	375 mL
¾ cup	granulated sugar	175 mL
2 tsp	baking powder	10 mL
1	egg	1
½ cup	milk	125 mL
⅓ cup	butter, melted	75 mL
1 cup	fresh or frozen raspberries	250 mL

Topping

¼ cup	packed brown sugar	60 mL
1 tbsp	all-purpose flour	15 mL
¼ cup	sliced almonds	60 mL
1 tbsp	butter, melted	15 mL

1. *Muffins:* In a large bowl, whisk together flour, sugar and baking powder. Set aside.

2. In a medium bowl, whisk together egg, milk and butter. Stir into flour mixture until just blended. Gently stir in raspberries.

3. *Topping:* In a small bowl, combine brown sugar, flour, almonds and butter.

4. If desired, place paper liners in wells. Fill each well with about 1½ tbsp (22 mL) batter. Sprinkle about 1 tsp (5 mL) topping over the batter in each well. Bake for 5 to 7 minutes or until a tester inserted in the center of a muffin comes out clean. Transfer muffins to a wire rack to cool. Repeat with the remaining batter and topping.

Tropical Muffins

**Makes
32 to 36 muffins**

This wonderful combination of pineapple and banana will make you dream of far-off islands and warm tropical breezes.

Tips

If you can't find a 15.5-oz (439 g) package of banana nut muffin mix, use 3⅓ cups (825 mL) banana muffin mix, or 3 cups (750 mL) banana muffin mix plus ½ cup (125 mL) chopped toasted walnuts or pecans.

If an 8-oz (227 mL) can of crushed pineapple isn't available, use a larger can and spoon pineapple and juice into a 1-cup (250 mL) measure, using close to same proportion of fruit and juice as in the can.

If desired, drizzle Vanilla Glaze (page 93) over these muffins and garnish with toasted coconut.

Store leftover muffins in an airtight container and plan to serve within a day or two. Or store in the freezer for up to 3 months.

- Paper liners (optional)

1	can (8 oz/227 mL) crushed pineapple, with juice	1
1	package (15.5 oz/439 g) banana nut muffin mix	1
1	egg	1
2 tbsp	vegetable oil	30 mL

1. Pour pineapple into a fine-mesh sieve set over a glass measuring cup. Press down lightly on fruit with the back of a spoon to drain well. Set fruit aside. Add enough water to the juice to equal ⅔ cup (150 mL). Set aside.

2. In a large bowl, whisk together muffin mix, egg and oil until blended. Stir in pineapple and juice.

3. If desired, place paper liners in wells. Fill each well with about 1½ tbsp (22 mL) batter. Bake for 6 to 8 minutes or until a tester inserted in the center of a muffin comes out clean. Transfer muffins to a wire rack to cool. Repeat with the remaining batter.

Pumpkin Streusel Muffins

**Makes
30 to 32 muffins**

We love teaching cooking classes together. As we teach the principles of baking and cooking, we laugh, tease each other and share stories. We brought this recipe to a Babycakes class, and the students swooned over the muffins.

Tips

Be sure to use solid packed canned pumpkin purée, not the sweetened, spiced pie filling in this recipe.

Store leftover muffins in an airtight container and plan to serve within a day or two. Or store in the freezer for up to 3 months.

• Paper liners (optional)

Muffins

2 cups	all-purpose flour	500 mL
1/2 cup	granulated sugar	125 mL
1/2 cup	packed brown sugar	125 mL
2 tsp	baking powder	10 mL
1 tsp	ground cinnamon	5 mL
1/2 tsp	salt	2 mL
1/2 tsp	ground ginger	2 mL
1/4 tsp	ground cloves	1 mL
1/4 tsp	ground nutmeg	1 mL
2	eggs	2
3/4 cup	canned pumpkin purée (not pie filling)	175 mL
1/2 cup	butter, melted and cooled slightly	125 mL
1/2 cup	sour cream	125 mL

Topping

1/3 cup	all-purpose flour	75 mL
1/4 cup	granulated sugar	60 mL
1/4 tsp	ground cinnamon	1 mL
1/4 cup	butter, softened	60 mL

1. *Muffins:* In a large bowl, whisk together flour, granulated sugar, brown sugar, baking powder, cinnamon, salt, ginger, cloves and nutmeg. Set aside.

2. In a medium bowl, whisk together eggs, pumpkin, butter and sour cream until blended. Stir into flour mixture until just blended.

3. *Topping:* In a small bowl, combine flour, sugar and cinnamon. Using a pastry blender or your fingers, cut in butter until crumbly and well combined.

4. If desired, place paper liners in wells. Fill each well with about 1 1/2 tbsp (22 mL) batter. Sprinkle about 1 1/2 tsp (7 mL) topping over the batter in each well. Bake for 5 to 7 minutes or until a tester inserted in the center of a muffin comes out clean. Transfer muffins to a wire rack to cool. Repeat with the remaining batter and topping.

Summertime Herb Muffins

**Makes
26 to 28 muffins**

With these muffins, you can enjoy fresh summer flavors all year long. Serve them for lunch with salad, or split them open and spread with flavored butter or cream cheese to serve as appetizers.

Tips

If desired, you can use 1½ tsp (7 mL) finely minced fresh rosemary in place of the dried.

Store leftover muffins in an airtight container and plan to serve within a day or two. Or store in the freezer for up to 3 months.

Variation

Omit the lemon zest and replace the rosemary with dried basil, oregano or thyme, or a combination. (Or use 1½ tsp/7 mL finely minced fresh herbs.)

- Paper liners (optional)

1½ cups	all-purpose flour	375 mL
¼ cup	granulated sugar	60 mL
2 tsp	baking powder	10 mL
1 tbsp	minced fresh flat-leaf (Italian) parsley	15 mL
½ tsp	dried rosemary, crushed	2 mL
½ tsp	salt	2 mL
1	egg	1
½ cup	milk	125 mL
¼ cup	vegetable oil	60 mL
½ tsp	grated lemon zest	2 mL

1. In a large bowl, whisk together flour, sugar, baking powder, parsley, rosemary and salt. Set aside.

2. In a medium bowl, whisk together egg, milk, oil and lemon zest until blended. Stir into flour mixture until just blended.

3. If desired, place paper liners in wells. Fill each well with about 1½ tbsp (22 mL) batter. Bake for 6 to 8 minutes or until a tester inserted in the center of a muffin comes out clean. Transfer muffins to a wire rack to cool. Repeat with the remaining batter.

Cheese and Jalapeño Corn Muffins

Makes 14 to 16 muffins

Cheddar cheese and jalapeño pepper add a flavor punch to cornbread muffins. Try them with Tex-Mex Butter (page 16).

Tips

If your cornbread mix contains a small amount of sugar (3 g per 34 g serving or less) and requires you to add oil, water and egg, rather than just egg and milk or water, use 1⅔ cups (400 mL) dry mix and add 2 tbsp (30 mL) granulated sugar and 3 tbsp (45 mL) vegetable oil with the egg.

While wonderful for lunch or supper, paired with a bowl of chili or stew, these muffins also make great appetizers or snacks. Split the muffins and spread lightly with softened cream cheese, a dollop of pepper jelly and a slice of cooked deli ham.

- Paper liners (optional)

1	package (8.5 oz/240 g) package corn muffin mix	1
1	small jalapeño pepper, seeded and minced	1
1	egg	1
⅓ cup	milk	75 mL
⅓ cup	sour cream	75 mL
½ cup	shredded Cheddar cheese	125 mL

1. In a medium bowl, whisk together muffin mix, jalapeño, egg, milk and sour cream until blended. Stir in cheese.

2. If desired, place paper liners in wells. Fill each well with about 1½ tbsp (22 mL) batter. Bake for 5 to 7 minutes or until a tester inserted in the center of a muffin comes out clean. Transfer muffins to a wire rack to cool slightly. Repeat with the remaining batter. Serve warm.

Ham and Parmesan Muffins

A simple meal —
maybe a soup or a
salad — becomes
something special
if you serve these
warm savory muffins
alongside.

Tip

These muffins are best
served fresh on the day
they are baked. If you
store leftovers for another
day, be sure to keep them
refrigerated in an airtight
container. Wrap in foil and
reheat in a 350°F (180°C)
oven or toaster oven for
5 minutes or until warm.

- Paper liners (optional)

1½ cups	all-purpose flour	375 mL
1½ tsp	baking powder	7 mL
1 tsp	dried basil	5 mL
¼ tsp	baking soda	1 mL
¼ tsp	salt	1 mL
¼ cup	freshly grated Parmesan cheese	60 mL
¼ cup	finely chopped cooked ham	60 mL
⅓ cup	butter, softened	75 mL
1 tbsp	granulated sugar	15 mL
1	egg	1
¾ cup	low-fat plain yogurt	175 mL
⅓ cup	milk	75 mL

1. In a medium bowl, whisk together flour, baking powder, basil, baking soda and salt. Stir in cheese and ham. Set aside.

2. In a large bowl, using an electric mixer on medium-high speed, beat butter and sugar for 1 to 2 minutes or until well blended. Add egg and beat for 1 minute. Beat in yogurt. Beat in milk. Stir in flour mixture until just blended.

3. If desired, place paper liners in wells. Fill each well with about 1½ tbsp (22 mL) batter. Bake for 5 to 7 minutes or until a tester inserted in the center of a muffin comes out clean. Transfer muffins to a wire rack to cool slightly. Repeat with the remaining batter. Serve warm.

Bacon Cheddar Muffins

**Makes
14 to 16 muffins**

Bacon may be a trendy ingredient right now, but these muffins are a classic. Cheese and bacon just naturally complement one another.

Tip

These muffins are best served while still warm or fresh on the day they are baked. If you store leftovers for another day, be sure to keep them refrigerated in an airtight container. Wrap in foil and reheat in a 350°F (180°C) oven or toaster oven for 5 minutes or until warm.

• Paper liners (optional)

1 cup	all-purpose flour	250 mL
2 tsp	granulated sugar	10 mL
1½ tsp	baking powder	7 mL
¼ tsp	salt	1 mL
1 cup	shredded sharp (old) Cheddar cheese	250 mL
¼ cup	crumbled crispy cooked bacon (about 4 slices)	60 mL
1	egg	1
½ cup	milk	125 mL
2 tbsp	butter, melted	30 mL

1. In a small bowl, whisk together flour, sugar, baking powder and salt. Stir in cheese and bacon. Set aside.

2. In a medium bowl, whisk together egg, milk and butter. Stir in flour mixture until just blended.

3. If desired, place paper liners in wells. Fill each well with about 1½ tbsp (22 mL) batter. Bake for 6 to 8 minutes or until a tester inserted in the center of a muffin comes out clean. Transfer muffins to a wire rack to cool slightly. Repeat with the remaining batter. Serve warm.

Crusts, Pies and Tarts

Favorite Pie Crust

Makes enough pastry for 8 two-crust hand pies or 16 single-crust mini pies

Roxanne's mother is a master pie baker. She has passed along her love of pies to Roxanne, and she has also shared her tried-and-true pie crust recipe with us.

Tips

The Babycakes cupcake maker comes with a two-piece pie crust tool set. The crust cutting tool looks like a double-sided cookie cutter, with one side slightly larger in diameter than the other. Use the large circle (about 3¼ inches/8 cm in diameter) to cut the bottom pie crust. Use the small circle (about 2⅞ inches/7 cm in diameter) to cut the top crust. The other piece in the set is the pie forming tool. You might think of it as the "pusher" — a little tool you can use to gently push the crust down into the well. It's perfect any time you are shaping a crust or cup.

If you have misplaced the crust cutting tool, you can use cookie cutters or biscuit cutters of about the same sizes.

• Blending fork or pastry blender

1⅓ cups	all-purpose flour	325 mL
½ tsp	salt	2 mL
½ cup	shortening	125 mL
4 to 5 tbsp	ice water	60 mL to 75 mL

1. In a large bowl, whisk together flour and salt. Using a blending fork or pastry blender, cut in shortening until mixture is crumbly. Add 4 tbsp (60 mL) ice water and let stand for 30 seconds. Blend with a fork until dough holds together and cleans the sides of the bowl, adding more ice water, if needed. Form dough into a disk, wrap in plastic wrap and refrigerate for at least 30 minutes or for up to 24 hours.

2. On a lightly floured surface, lightly dust top of dough with flour. Roll out gently, picking dough up after each roll and rotating it from 12 o'clock to 3 o'clock. (This keeps the dough from sticking.) Roll and rotate until dough is about ⅛ inch (3 mm) thick.

3. Use as directed in the recipe, or follow these baking directions to adapt your own recipes.

To Bake Two-Crust Hand Pies

Use the large circle of the crust cutting tool to cut 8 bottom crusts, and use the small circle to cut 8 top crusts, rerolling scraps as necessary. Place large crusts evenly on top of wells and gently press into wells with the pie forming tool. Spoon filling into each bottom crust until about half full. Place small crusts directly over the center of each filled shell. For added browning and sheen, lightly whisk together 1 egg and 1 tbsp (15 mL) water and brush lightly over top crusts. Bake for 12 to 15 minutes or until top crusts are golden brown and crisp. Transfer pies to a wire rack to cool.

Tips

Wrap leftover dough tightly in plastic wrap and refrigerate; use within 3 days or freeze for up to 2 months. Let thaw overnight in the refrigerator, then roll out and use as desired.

For a flakier crust, use pastry flour instead of all-purpose flour.

To Bake Single-Crust Mini Pies

Use the large circle of the crust cutting tool to cut 8 crusts. Place crusts evenly on top of wells and gently press into wells with the pie forming tool. If desired, crimp the top edge. Spoon 1 to 2 tbsp (15 to 30 mL) filling into each crust. Bake for 10 to 12 minutes or until filling is cooked according to recipe directions and crusts are golden brown. Transfer pies to a wire rack to cool.

To Bake Single Crusts Blind (Empty)

Use the large circle of the crust cutting tool to cut 8 crusts. Place crusts evenly on top of wells and gently press into wells with the pie forming tool. If desired, crimp the top edge. Evenly prick the bottom and around the sides of each crust with the tines of a fork, being careful not to scratch the surface of the wells. Bake for 8 to 10 minutes or until crusts are golden and crisp. Transfer crusts to a wire rack to cool. Fill the cooled pie crusts with any of the fillings in this book, or, for a quick filling, spoon in prepared pudding, mousse, fruit, jam or ice cream.

If the pastry crust recipe you are preparing has a tendency to puff while baking, prick the crust, then line each crust with a paper liner or a small circle of parchment paper or foil and fill it with dry beans. First, spray the outside bottom of the liner, paper or foil with nonstick baking spray, to prevent the liner from sticking to the crusts. Once you've added the beans, bake as directed above, then gently remove paper or foil from crusts. Be sure you get each and every bean — no one would want to bite into a hard, dry bean instead of a creamy, wonderful pie. Beans that have been baked in a pie crust should not be used for cooking. Let them cool thoroughly, then place in a jar or ziplock bag and use again as pie weights.

Pizza Crusts

These fun, crisp little cups make perfect crusts for bite-size pizzas.

Tips

Try Italian Sausage Pizza Bites (page 156) or Fresh Tomato Pizza Bites (page 193), or use your favorite pizza toppings as fillings, using one of our recipes as a guideline to proportions.

If the pizza crust puffs, carefully use the pie forming tool to push down gently on the crust before filling.

If you have misplaced the crust cutting tool, you can use a cookie cutter about 3¼ inches (8 cm) in diameter.

• **Food processor**

1 cup	all-purpose flour	250 mL
1 tsp	quick-rise yeast	5 mL
½ tsp	salt	2 mL
1 tsp	olive oil	5 mL
⅓ cup	warm water	75 mL
	Pizza fillings as desired (see tip, at left)	

1. In a food processor fitted with a metal blade, combine flour, yeast and salt; process for 30 seconds. With the motor running, through the feed tube, gradually add oil, then warm water, and process until a dough forms.

2. Transfer to a floured surface and form into a ball. Cover loosely with plastic wrap and let rest for 10 minutes.

3. Keeping surface lightly floured, roll out dough into a very thin rectangle, about 13- by 8-inches (33 by 20 cm). Use the large circle of the crust cutting tool to cut 8 crusts. Place crusts evenly on top of wells and gently press into wells with the pie forming tool.

4. Bake for 7 minutes or until crust is set and beginning to dry. Evenly spoon filling into each parbaked crust. Bake for 5 to 7 minutes or until filling is hot and crusts are crisp. Transfer crusts to a wire rack to cool slightly.

Phyllo Cups

Fresh and wonderfully crisp phyllo cups can't be beat. They are so easy to make — and they are made without butter. What more could you ask for?

Tips

Different brands of phyllo dough come in different-size sheets. For this recipe, we used 20 sheets that are 14 by 9 inches (35 by 23 cm), which is about half of a 16-oz (454 g) package. Some sheets are larger (17 by 12 inches/43 by 30 cm or 18 by 14 inches/ 45 by 35 cm), so use 10 and cut them in half crosswise before folding as directed in step 1.

Store cooled baked phyllo cups in an airtight container at room temperature for 1 to 2 days.

Bake the entire roll of phyllo dough, seal any extra cups in an airtight container and freeze for up to 2 months.

20	sheets frozen phyllo dough, thawed (see tip, at left)	20
	Nonstick baking spray	

1. Place 1 sheet of phyllo on a cutting board. (Immediately cover the remaining phyllo sheets with plastic wrap and then a lightly dampened towel, keeping them covered to prevent them from drying out.) Fold the sheet into thirds, making a 9- by $4\frac{1}{2}$-inch (23 by 11 cm) rectangle. Fold the rectangle in half, making a $4\frac{1}{2}$-inch (11 cm) square.

2. Using the large circle of the crust cutting tool, imprint a circle into the phyllo, pressing firmly. Using kitchen shears, cut out the circle (discard scraps). Place the stack (there will be 6 layers) on top of a well and very gently press into well with the pie forming tool, making a cup. Repeat with 7 more sheets of phyllo until all 8 wells are covered. Spray the inside of each cup with baking spray.

3. Bake for 5 to 7 minutes or until phyllo cups are crisp. Transfer cups to a wire rack to cool slightly. Repeat with the remaining phyllo sheets.

Toast Cups

Old-fashioned and yet trendy and new at the same time, toast cups are the perfect edible bowl for appetizers, sandwich fillings, breakfast fillings and so much more.

Tips

Make lunch special for your children — they will get a kick out of these toast cups filled with cheese, peanut butter and jelly or any favorite filling.

For appetizers, fill toast cups with dip, chicken or seafood salad, or creamed shrimp or crab. Hot or cold, they will be the hit of the party.

For smaller toast cups, use the small circle of the crust cutting tool.

Variation

Use any variety of soft, fresh bread, such as whole wheat or sourdough.

8	slices white bread	8
2 tsp	butter, softened, or spreadable margarine	10 mL

1. Using a rolling pin, roll each slice of bread until it is very thin. Use the large circle of the crust cutting tool to cut a circle from each slice (discard scraps or reserve for another use). Spread one side of each circle with butter.

2. Place 1 bread circle, buttered side down, on top of each well and gently press into well with the pie forming tool, making a cup.

3. Bake for 6 to 8 minutes or until toast cups are crisp and golden brown. Transfer cups to a wire rack to cool slightly.

Crescent Roll Cups

How many fillings can you think of to serve in these cups? The possibilities are endless! For a start, try tuna salad, cheesy cooked broccoli or a small fresh salad.

Tips

For a quick sweet snack, bake crescent roll cups as directed, then fill each hot cup (still in Babycakes) with a few chocolate chips or a small spoonful of hazelnut spread and a few toasted chopped nuts. Bake for 1 minute or just until chocolate melts or spread is heated through.

If you have misplaced the crust cutting tool, you can use a cookie cutter about $2\frac{7}{8}$ inches (7 cm) in diameter.

1	can (8 oz/227 g) refrigerated crescent roll dough	1

1. Carefully unroll crescent roll dough in one piece. Press seams together to make 1 rectangular piece of dough. Using a rolling pin, roll out dough to about $\frac{1}{8}$ inch (3 mm) thick. Using the small circle of the crust cutting tool, cut 12 circles, rerolling scraps as necessary.

2. Place 1 dough circle on top of each well and gently press into well with the pie forming tool, making a cup. (You will have 4 circles left over.)

3. Bake for 2 minutes. If the dough has puffed, carefully press down on it with the pie forming tool so it stays in a cup shape. Bake for 3 to 4 minutes or until cups are golden brown. Carefully transfer cups to a wire rack to cool. Repeat with the remaining dough circles, being careful not to burn yourself on the hot plates.

Tortilla Cups

**Makes
28 cups**

You will find endless uses for these Mexican-inspired cups. Think outside the shell!

Tips

Warming the tortillas one at a time in the microwave just as you are ready to cut and shape them ensures that they stay pliable.

Deep-fry the leftover tortilla scraps to use in salads.

4	10-inch (25 cm) flour tortillas	4

1. Working with 1 tortilla at a time, wrap tortilla in a paper towel and microwave on High for about 20 seconds or just until warm. Using the large circle of the crust cutting tool, cut 7 circles from the warm tortilla (discard scraps or reserve for another use).

2. Place 1 tortilla circle on top of each well and very gently press into well with the pie forming tool, making a cup.

3. Bake for 5 to 6 minutes or until tortilla cups are crisp. Transfer cups to a wire rack to cool. Repeat with the remaining tortillas.

Tip

To make enough for a party or a larger family, bake up several batches of tortilla cups and place them on a baking sheet. Keep them warm in a 250°F (120°C) oven until ready to serve, for up to 20 minutes. Alternatively, let cool and store at room temperature for up to 4 hours. Just before serving, reheat in a 250°F (120°C) oven for about 10 minutes.

Wonton Cups

**Makes
8 cups**

You'll have such fun loading these Asian-inspired cups with dips and fillings.

Tip

For a more rustic look, place the whole wonton wrapper (not a cut circle) in the well. The ruffled edges will brown and crisp, and will make a nice holder to grasp as you are enjoying the filled cup.

8	wonton wrappers (about 3½ inches/ 8.5 cm square)	8

1. Use the large circle of the crust cutting tool to cut a circle from each wonton wrapper (discard scraps).

2. Place 1 wonton circle on top of each well and gently press down into well with the pie forming tool, making a cup.

3. Bake for 6 to 8 minutes or until crisp. Transfer cups to a wire rack to cool.

Mile-High Chocolate Cream Pies

Roxanne's husband, Bob, doesn't request many recipes, but this pie is his number one pick for special occasions. The flavor of the deep fudge filling will make it a top 10 favorite at your home, too!

Tips

Filled tarts can be loosely covered and refrigerated for up to 24 hours before adding topping.

If using a store-bought refrigerated pie crust, let come to room temperature, then unroll according to package directions and proceed with the recipe. You can cut 14 Babycakes single crusts from one packaged pie crust (half a 14-oz/400 g package) by rerolling the scraps.

Variation

Mile-High Chocolate Meringue Pie: Prepare this recipe through step 2, then dollop on the meringue topping from Lemon Meringue Mini Pies (page 124) and proceed with step 5 from that recipe.

Crusts

	Favorite Pie Crust (page 114) or store-bought refrigerated pie crust (see tip, at left)	

Filling

1/2 cup	granulated sugar	125 mL
1/4 cup	all-purpose flour	60 mL
2 tbsp	unsweetened cocoa powder	30 mL
Pinch	salt	Pinch
2	egg yolks, lightly beaten	2
1 cup	milk	250 mL
2 tbsp	butter	30 mL
1/2 tsp	vanilla extract	2 mL

Topping

1/2 cup	heavy or whipping (35%) cream	125 mL
1 1/2 tbsp	confectioners' (icing) sugar	22 mL

1. *Crusts:* Follow the instructions on page 115 for baking single crusts blind.

2. *Filling:* In a medium saucepan, whisk together sugar, flour, cocoa and salt. Whisk in egg yolks, milk and butter. Bring to a boil over medium heat, whisking constantly. Boil, whisking constantly, for about 1 minute or until thickened. Remove from heat and stir in vanilla. Spoon into baked crusts, piling high. Let cool at room temperature for about 1 hour, until filling is set.

3. *Topping:* Just before serving, in a medium bowl, using an electric mixer on high speed, beat whipping cream and confectioners' sugar until stiff. Dollop on pies.

Southern Pecan Pie Bliss

**Makes
8 mini pies**

Roxanne loves the food traditions of the southern United States, where this pie is popular. It must be an inherited family trait, as pecan pie is her dad's favorite all year long.

Tips

Toasting pecans intensifies their flavor. Spread chopped pecans in a single layer on a baking sheet. Bake at 350°F (180°C) for 5 to 7 minutes or until lightly browned. Let cool, then measure.

Top pies with sweetened whipped cream, if desired. In a small bowl, using an electric mixer on high speed, beat ½ cup (125 mL) heavy or whipping (35%) cream until frothy. Beat in 1 tbsp (15 mL) confectioners' (icing) sugar until stiff peaks form. Dollop or pipe sweetened whipped cream on top of each pie.

Variation

Stir ⅓ cup (75 mL) mini semisweet chocolate chips into the pie filling with the pecans. The pies will be just a little fuller.

Crusts

	Favorite Pie Crust (page 114) or store-bought refrigerated pie crust (see tip, page 123)	

Filling

¼ cup	packed brown sugar	60 mL
¼ tsp	salt	1 mL
1	egg, beaten	1
2 tbsp	dark (golden) corn syrup	30 mL
1 tbsp	butter, melted	15 mL
¾ cup	chopped pecans, toasted (see tip, at left)	175 mL

1. *Crusts:* Use the large circle of the crust cutting tool to cut 8 crusts. Place crusts evenly on top of wells and gently press into wells with the pie forming tool. If desired, crimp the top edge.

2. *Filling:* In a medium bowl, whisk together brown sugar, salt, egg, corn syrup and butter until well blended. Stir in pecans. Spoon about 2 tbsp (30 mL) filling into each crust.

3. Bake for 10 to 12 minutes or until crusts are golden brown and a tester inserted in the center of the pie comes out clean. Transfer pies to a wire rack to cool.

Pecan Toffee Tassies

Are you a pecan pie lover? This recipe gilds the lily. The addition of chocolate-covered toffee candy bars makes these pies hard to beat.

Tips

Make these ahead and freeze for easy holiday entertaining. To freeze, let pies cool completely, then place in an airtight container and freeze for up to 3 months.

If using a store-bought refrigerated pie crust, let come to room temperature, then unroll according to package directions and proceed with the recipe. You can cut 14 Babycakes single crusts from one packaged pie crust (half a 14-oz/400 g package) by rerolling the scraps.

Crusts

	Favorite Pie Crust (page 114) or store-bought refrigerated pie crust (see tip, at left)	

Filling

½ cup	packed brown sugar	125 mL
1 tbsp	all-purpose flour	15 mL
1	egg, beaten	1
2 tbsp	butter, melted	30 mL
1 tsp	vanilla extract	5 mL
½ cup	chopped pecans, toasted (see tip, page 122)	125 mL
2	chocolate-covered toffee candy bars, such as Skor or Heath (each 1.4 oz/39 g), crushed into small pieces (about ½ cup/125 mL)	2

1. *Crusts:* Use the large circle of the crust cutting tool to cut 10 to 12 crusts. Place 8 crusts evenly on top of wells and gently press into wells with the pie forming tool. Cover the remaining crusts with plastic wrap.

2. *Filling:* In a medium bowl, whisk together brown sugar, flour, egg, butter and vanilla until well blended. Stir in pecans and crushed candy. Spoon about 2 tbsp (30 mL) filling into each crust.

3. Bake for 10 to 12 minutes or until filling is set and crusts are golden brown. Transfer pies to a wire rack to cool.

4. Unplug Babycakes and let cool for 5 minutes. Plug back in and repeat with the remaining crusts and filling.

Lemon Meringue Mini Pies

· ·

**Makes
8 mini pies**

Kathy's mother's
favorite pie was lemon
meringue, and they
shared one every
Mother's Day and on
her mother's birthday
instead of cake. Don't
wait for a special
holiday to enjoy these
delightful miniature
versions.

· ·

Tip

Some restaurants and
bakeries prepare their
meringues "mile high,"
and now you can make
"mile-high" minis at home.
Use 2 egg whites (at room
temperature), ¼ tsp (1 mL)
cream of tartar and ¼ cup
(60 mL) granulated sugar,
and beat as directed in
step 3. Generously spoon
or pipe meringue onto
each pie, piling high in the
center. Bake as directed in
step 5.

• **Preheat oven to 375°F (190°C)**

Crusts

	Favorite Pie Crust (page 114) or store-bought refrigerated pie crust (see tip, page 123)	

Filling

½ cup	granulated sugar	125 mL
2 tbsp	cornstarch	30 mL
Pinch	salt	Pinch
3	egg yolks, beaten	3
½ cup	cold water	125 mL
	Grated zest of 1 lemon	
6 tbsp	freshly squeezed lemon juice	90 mL
1 tbsp	butter	15 mL

Meringue

1	egg white, at room temperature	1
⅛ tsp	cream of tartar	0.5 mL
2 tbsp	granulated sugar	30 mL

1. *Crusts:* Follow the instructions on page 115 for baking single crusts blind.

2. *Filling:* In a small saucepan, combine sugar, cornstarch and salt. Stir in egg yolks until blended. Stir in cold water until thoroughly combined. Cook over medium-low heat, stirring constantly, for 7 to 9 minutes or until mixture bubbles and thickens. Remove from heat and add lemon zest, lemon juice and butter, stirring until smooth. Set aside.

3. *Meringue:* In a small, deep bowl, using an electric mixer on high speed, beat egg white until frothy. Beat in cream of tartar. Gradually beat in sugar until stiff peaks form.

4. Spoon filling into baked crusts, dividing equally. Spoon or pipe a dollop of meringue on top of each. Place pies on a baking sheet.

5. Bake in preheated oven for 5 to 7 minutes or until meringue is light golden brown. Transfer pies to a wire rack to cool.

Old-Fashioned Cherry Hand Pies

Makes 8 hand pies

Mention cherry pie and most people think of dinner at Grandma's or of the neighbor's cherry tree. But alumni of Iowa State University, such as Kathy's daughter, recall the spring festival VEISHEA, where they make, sell and eat over 10,000 tiny cherry pies, a tradition since the 1920s. While the Iowa State pies are single-crust pies topped with whipped cream, we decided to go double-crust with our version.

Tips

There is no need to thaw the cherries.

The filling can be prepared 1 day ahead and refrigerated in an airtight container.

If you're short on time, replace the filling with ¾ cup (175 mL) canned cherry pie filling (or any other flavor).

Variation

To make single-crust cherry pies, follow the instructions on page 115 for baking single crusts blind. Spoon the filling into the baked crusts and top with whipped cream.

Filling

1¼ cups	frozen pitted tart cherries	300 mL
½ cup	granulated sugar	125 mL
4 tsp	cornstarch	20 mL
1 tbsp	water	15 mL
½ tsp	freshly squeezed lemon juice	2 mL
¼ tsp	almond extract	1 mL

Crusts

	Favorite Pie Crust (page 114) or store-bought refrigerated pie crust (see tip, page 126)	
1	egg	1
1 tbsp	water	15 mL

1. *Filling:* In a small saucepan, combine cherries and sugar. Cook over medium-low heat, stirring frequently, for 11 to 12 minutes or until boiling and cherries are tender.

2. In a small bowl, whisk together cornstarch and water until smooth. Stir into cherry mixture and cook, stirring constantly, for 2 to 3 minutes or until liquid is glossy and mixture is thickened. Remove from heat and stir in lemon juice and almond extract. Spoon into a small bowl and let cool completely.

3. *Crusts:* Use the large circle of the crust cutting tool to cut 8 bottom crusts, and use the small circle to cut 8 top crusts, rerolling scraps as necessary. Place large crusts evenly on top of wells and gently press into wells with the pie forming tool.

4. Spoon 1½ tbsp (22 mL) filling into each bottom crust. Place small crusts directly over the center of each filled shell.

5. In a small bowl, whisk together egg and water. Brush lightly over top crusts.

6. Bake for 12 to 15 minutes or until crusts are browned and crisp. Transfer pies to a wire rack to cool.

Cranberry Tassies

A drizzle of white chocolate adds an elegant touch to a holiday classic.

Tips

For easy drizzling, spoon melted white chocolate into a sealable food storage bag and snip off one corner.

Substitute chopped walnuts for the pecans.

If using a store-bought refrigerated pie crust, let come to room temperature, then unroll according to package directions and proceed with the recipe. You can cut 14 Babycakes single crusts from one packaged pie crust (half a 14-oz/400 g package) by rerolling the scraps.

Filling

1/3 cup	sweetened dried cranberries	75 mL
1/2 cup	water	125 mL
2 tbsp	orange marmalade	30 mL
2 tbsp	chopped pecans	30 mL

Crusts

Favorite Pie Crust (page 114) or store-bought refrigerated pie crust (see tip, at left)

Topping

2 oz	white chocolate, chopped	60 g

1. *Filling:* In a small saucepan, combine cranberries and water. Bring to a boil over medium-high heat. Remove from heat and let stand for 3 minutes; drain excess liquid. Stir in marmalade and pecans.

2. *Crusts:* Use the large circle of the crust cutting tool to cut 8 crusts. Place crusts evenly on top of wells and gently press into wells with the pie forming tool.

3. Spoon filling into crusts, dividing equally. Bake for 10 to 12 minutes or until filling is hot and crust is golden brown. Transfer pies to a wire rack and let cool for 15 minutes.

4. *Topping:* Place white chocolate in a small microwave-safe glass bowl. Microwave on High in 30-second intervals, stirring after each, until chocolate is melted and smooth. Drizzle over pies.

Fresh Strawberry Mini Pies

**Makes
8 mini pies**

Fresh strawberries and warm days just go together, and these mini pies are a wonderful way to serve the succulent berries. One of our favorite ideas for a dessert flight is to serve these beauties with a couple of types of fun cupcakes.

Tips

If desired, garnish the top of each pie with a small whole strawberry.

You can substitute 1/4 cup (60 mL) strawberry preserves or jam for the chopped strawberry mixture. Spoon preserves into a small microwave-safe glass bowl and microwave on High for 15 to 20 seconds or until melted. Stir in sliced strawberries and proceed with the recipe.

Crusts

	Favorite Pie Crust (page 114) or store-bought refrigerated pie crust (see tip, page 126)	

Filling

1 1/4 cups	small strawberries, divided	300 mL
2 tbsp	granulated sugar	30 mL
1/2 tsp	cornstarch	2 mL
1/2 tsp	freshly squeezed lemon juice	2 mL

Topping

1/2 cup	heavy or whipping (35%) cream	125 mL
1 tbsp	confectioners' (icing) sugar	15 mL

1. *Crusts:* Follow the instructions on page 115 for baking single crusts blind.

2. *Filling:* Finely chop 1/4 cup (60 mL) of the strawberries. Place in a small microwave-safe glass bowl and mash with the back of a spoon to release some juice. Stir in sugar, cornstarch and lemon juice. Microwave on High for 1 minute. Stir well and microwave for 30 seconds or until juices are boiling. Let cool slightly.

3. Thinly slice the remaining strawberries. Add to chopped strawberry mixture and toss gently to coat. Spoon filling into baked crusts, dividing equally.

4. *Topping:* In a small bowl, using an electric mixer on high speed, beat cream until frothy. Beat in confectioners' sugar until stiff peaks form. Dollop or pipe onto pies.

Fruit Preserves Hand Pies

. . . .

**Makes
8 hand pies**

Warning: These hand
pies are addictive!
Roxanne likes to
fill each pie with a
different preserve,
jam or jelly, then
let her family select
their favorites.

. . . .

Tips

If using a store-bought
refrigerated pie crust, let
come to room temperature,
then unroll according to
package directions and
proceed with the recipe.
If you roll the dough thin
enough, you can cut
8 Babycakes two-crust
pie crusts from one 14-oz
(400 g) package.

Have fun and use any of
your favorite preserves,
jams or jellies.

Crusts

Favorite Pie Crust (page 114) or
store-bought refrigerated pie crust
(see tip, at left)

Filling

1/3 cup	apricot or strawberry preserves, jelly or jam	75 mL
1	egg	1
1 tbsp	water	15 mL

1. *Crusts:* Use the large circle of the crust cutting tool to cut 8 bottom crusts, and use the small circle to cut 8 top crusts, rerolling scraps as necessary. Place large crusts evenly on top of wells and gently press into wells with the pie forming tool.

2. *Filling:* Spoon about 2 tsp (10 mL) preserves into each bottom crust. Place small crusts directly over the center of each filled shell.

3. In a small bowl, whisk together egg and water. Brush lightly over top crusts.

4. Bake for 12 to 15 minutes or until crusts are browned and crisp. Transfer pies to a wire rack to cool.

Pumpkin Mini Pies

There's no need to wait until Thanksgiving to enjoy pumpkin pie. These mini delights are so easy you can indulge all year long.

Tips

If using a store-bought refrigerated pie crust, let come to room temperature, then unroll according to package directions and proceed with the recipe. You can cut 14 Babycakes single crusts from one packaged pie crust (half a 14-oz/400 g package) by rerolling the scraps.

Leftover canned pumpkin purée? Store it in an airtight container in the refrigerator for up to 1 week or in the freezer for up to 3 months. Thaw overnight in the refrigerator, and stir well before using.

Crusts

	Favorite Pie Crust (page 114) or store-bought refrigerated pie crust (see tip, at left)	

Filling

3 tbsp	granulated sugar	45 mL
1/2 tsp	pumpkin pie spice	2 mL
1/4 tsp	salt	1 mL
1	egg	1
1/3 cup	canned pumpkin purée (not pie filling)	75 mL
1/3 cup	heavy or whipping (35%) cream	75 mL

Topping

1/2 cup	heavy or whipping (35%) cream	125 mL
1 tbsp	confectioners' (icing) sugar	15 mL

1. *Crusts:* Use the large circle of the crust cutting tool to cut 8 crusts. Place crusts evenly on top of wells and gently press into wells with the pie forming tool.

2. *Filling:* In a medium bowl, whisk together sugar, pumpkin pie spice, salt, egg, pumpkin and cream until blended. Spoon 1 1/2 to 2 tbsp (22 to 30 mL) filling into each crust.

3. Bake for 8 to 10 minutes or until filling is set and a tester inserted in the center of a pie comes out clean. Transfer pies to a wire rack to cool.

4. *Topping:* In a small bowl, using an electric mixer on high speed, beat cream until frothy. Beat in confectioners' sugar until stiff peaks form. Dollop or pipe onto pies.

Chocolate Peanut Butter Tarts

Makes 8 tarts

Certain things just go together. You're sure to love the timeless combination of chocolate and peanut butter in these mini tarts.

Tips

Use a food processor fitted with a metal blade to quickly make fine crumbs from the cookies. You'll need about 6 cream-filled chocolate sandwich cookies (such as Oreos) to make ½ cup (125 mL) crumbs.

Garnish tarts with chopped chocolate peanut butter cup candies, chopped dry-roasted peanuts or chocolate-covered peanuts.

Use a small offset spatula to lift the tarts from the wells. Be careful not to scrape the coating on the cupcake maker.

- Paper liners

Crusts

½ cup	cream-filled chocolate sandwich cookie crumbs	125 mL
1 tbsp	butter, melted	15 mL

Filling

2 tbsp	packed brown sugar	30 mL
2 tsp	all-purpose flour	10 mL
Pinch	salt	Pinch
¼ cup	creamy peanut butter	60 mL
¼ cup	light (white or golden) corn syrup	60 mL
1	egg	1

Topping

¼ cup	semisweet chocolate chips	60 mL
1 tbsp	butter	15 mL
1 tbsp	light (white or golden) corn syrup	15 mL

1. *Crusts:* Place paper liners in wells. In a small bowl, combine cookie crumbs and butter. Place about 1½ tsp (7 mL) in the bottom of each liner, tapping it in with the pie forming tool.

2. *Filling:* In a medium bowl, using an electric mixer on medium speed, beat brown sugar, flour, salt, peanut butter and corn syrup for 30 seconds or until combined. Beat in egg. Spoon about 1 to 1½ tbsp (15 to 22 mL) filling onto each crust.

3. Bake for 8 to 10 minutes or until a tester inserted in the center of the filling comes out clean. Using a small offset spatula, carefully transfer tarts to a wire rack to cool.

4. *Topping:* In a small microwave-safe glass bowl, combine chocolate chips, butter and corn syrup. Microwave on High for 30 seconds. Stir until blended and thick. Drizzle about 1½ tsp (7 mL) topping over each tart.

Canadian Butter Tarts

**Makes
8 tarts**

These may be a traditional Canadian treat, but we think they should become a favorite across the United States, too. Once you taste them, we're sure you'll agree.

Variation

Omit the raisins and boiling water, and melt the butter. In a medium bowl, combine ¼ cup (60 mL) toasted chopped pecans and melted butter. Stir in the brown sugar and corn syrup, then proceed with the recipe.

Filling

¼ cup	raisins	60 mL
½ cup	boiling water	125 mL
2 tbsp	butter, cut into small cubes and softened	30 mL
¼ cup	packed brown sugar	60 mL
2 tbsp	dark (golden) corn syrup	30 mL
2	egg yolks, beaten	2
½ tsp	vanilla extract	2 mL
½ tsp	freshly squeezed lemon juice	2 mL

Crusts

Favorite Pie Crust (page 114) or store-bought refrigerated pie crust (see tip, page 129)

1. *Filling:* Place raisins in a medium bowl and cover with boiling water. Let stand for 10 minutes. Drain and return raisins to bowl. Stir in butter until it begins to melt. Stir in brown sugar and corn syrup until well combined and butter has melted. Stir in egg yolks, vanilla and lemon juice.

2. *Crusts:* Use the large circle of the crust cutting tool to cut 8 crusts. Place crusts evenly on top of wells and gently press into wells with the pie forming tool.

3. Spoon about 1½ tbsp (22 mL) filling into each crust. Bake for 11 to 13 minutes or until crust is browned and crisp and a tester inserted in the center of a tart comes out clean. Transfer tarts to a wire rack and let cool for 10 minutes.

Caramel Tarts

· ·

**Makes
8 tarts**

These rich little tarts
are big on flavor and
make the perfect
dessert.

· ·

Variation

Caramel Nut Tart: Stir
¼ cup (60 mL) salted
cashew halves or dry-
roasted peanuts into the
filling just before spooning
it into the crusts.

Crusts

Favorite Pie Crust (page 114) or
store-bought refrigerated pie crust
(see tip, page 133)

Filling

½ cup	packed brown sugar	125 mL
2 tbsp	butter	30 mL
¼ cup	heavy or whipping (35%) cream	60 mL
1 tsp	vanilla extract	5 mL
5	soft caramel candies	5

1. *Crusts:* Follow the instructions on page 115 for baking
   single crusts blind.

2. *Filling:* In a small saucepan, combine brown sugar
   and butter. Cook over medium heat, stirring often,
   for 2 minutes or until butter is melted and sugar is
   dissolved. Stir in cream and cook, stirring constantly,
   for 2 minutes. Remove from heat and immediately stir
   in caramels. Let stand, stirring occasionally, for about
   10 minutes or until caramels are melted.

3. Spoon about 1½ tbsp (22 mL) filling into each baked
   crust and let stand for about 1 hour to cool and
   thicken.

Coconut Cream Tarts

**Makes
8 tarts**

If you haven't enjoyed
the taste of coconut
cream pie in a while,
now is the time!

Tip

If using a store-bought
refrigerated pie crust, let
come to room temperature,
then unroll according to
package directions and
proceed with the recipe.
You can cut 14 Babycakes
single crusts from one
packaged pie crust (half a
14-oz/400 g package) by
rerolling the scraps.

Crusts

	Favorite Pie Crust (page 114) or store-bought refrigerated pie crust (see tip, at left)	

Filling

¼ cup	granulated sugar	60 mL
1½ tbsp	cornstarch	22 mL
Pinch	salt	Pinch
1	egg yolk, lightly beaten	1
1 cup	milk	250 mL
5 tbsp	sweetened flaked coconut, divided	75 mL
1½ tsp	butter	7 mL
½ tsp	vanilla extract	2 mL

Topping

½ cup	heavy or whipping (35%) cream	125 mL
1 tbsp	confectioners' (icing) sugar	15 mL

1. *Crusts:* Follow the instructions on page 115 for baking single crusts blind.

2. *Filling:* In a small saucepan, whisk together sugar, cornstarch and salt. Whisk in egg yolk and milk. Bring to a boil over medium heat, whisking constantly. Boil, whisking constantly, for about 1 minute or until thickened. Remove from heat and stir in 3 tbsp (45 mL) of the coconut, butter and vanilla.

3. Spoon about 2 tbsp (30 mL) filling into each baked crust. Refrigerate for about 1 hour or until chilled.

4. Meanwhile, preheat oven to 350°F (180°C). Spread the remaining coconut on a baking sheet. Bake for 5 to 7 minutes or until golden and lightly toasted.

5. *Topping:* In a small bowl, using an electric mixer on high speed, beat cream until frothy. Beat in confectioners' sugar until stiff peaks form. Dollop or pipe onto pies. Garnish with toasted coconut.

Rustic Apple Strudel Tarts

Makes 8 tarts

Sometimes it seems you can taste something in your mind forever. For Kathy, the incredible taste of an apple strudel purchased at an open booth on the streets of Frankfurt, Germany, is one of those memories. We've captured that flavor in these tarts.

Tips

Toasting walnuts intensifies their flavor. Spread chopped walnuts in a single layer on a baking sheet. Bake at 350°F (180°C) for 5 to 7 minutes or until lightly browned. Let cool, then measure.

If desired, dollop sweetened whipped cream on each tart. To make sweetened whipped cream, in a small bowl, using an electric mixer on high speed, beat ½ cup (125 mL) heavy or whipping (35%) cream until frothy. Add 1 tbsp (15 mL) confectioner's (icing) sugar and beat until stiff.

1 tbsp	butter	15 mL
1	Granny Smith or other tart cooking apple, peeled and finely chopped (about 1 cup/250 mL)	1
2 tbsp	golden raisins	30 mL
2 tbsp	granulated sugar	30 mL
½ tsp	ground cinnamon	2 mL
2 tbsp	water, divided	30 mL
1 tsp	freshly squeezed lemon juice	5 mL
Pinch	salt	Pinch
½ tsp	cornstarch	2 mL
¼ cup	chopped toasted walnuts (see tip, at left)	60 mL
8	baked Phyllo Cups (page 117)	8

1. In a small saucepan, melt butter over medium-low heat. Add apple, raisins, sugar, cinnamon, 1 tbsp (15 mL) of the water and lemon juice. Cook, stirring frequently, for 8 to 9 minutes or until apple is tender.

2. In a small bowl, combine cornstarch and the remaining water. Stir into apple mixture and cook, stirring constantly, for about 2 minutes or until juices bubble and thicken. Stir in walnuts.

3. Spoon about 1 heaping tbsp (15 mL) apple mixture into each phyllo cup. Serve immediately.

Peach Hand Tarts

Reminiscent of
Southern fried pies
but without the hassle
of frying, these tarts
are just the right
size for indulgence
without guilt!

Tips

If desired, stir 2 tbsp (30 mL)
toasted chopped pecans
into the filling just before
spooning it into the crusts.

If using a store-bought
refrigerated pie crust, let
come to room temperature,
then unroll according to
package directions and
proceed with the recipe.
If you roll the dough thin
enough, you can cut
8 Babycakes two-crust
pie crusts from one 14-oz
(400 g) package.

Filling

¾ cup	dried peaches, cut into small pieces	175 mL
¼ cup	granulated sugar	60 mL
Pinch	ground cinnamon	Pinch
Pinch	ground nutmeg	Pinch
½ cup	water	125 mL

Crusts

Favorite Pie Crust (page 114) or
store-bought refrigerated pie crust
(see tip, at left)

1. *Filling:* In a small saucepan, combine peaches, sugar,
   cinnamon, nutmeg and water. Bring to a boil over
   medium-high heat. Reduce heat and simmer, stirring
   occasionally, for 20 minutes. Remove from heat and
   mash with a potato masher or fork.

2. *Crusts:* Use the large circle of the crust cutting tool
   to cut 8 bottom crusts, and use the small circle to cut
   8 top crusts, rerolling scraps as necessary. Place large
   crusts evenly on top of wells and gently press into the
   wells with the pie forming tool.

3. Spoon filling into bottom crusts, dividing equally.
   Place small crusts directly over the center of each
   filled shell.

4. Bake for 12 to 15 minutes or until crusts are browned
   and crisp. Transfer tarts to a wire rack to cool.

Part 3

All-Day, Any Day

Breakfast and Brunch

Baked Eggs

Roxanne's house can get harried in the mornings as everyone rushes to get ready for work or school. But she is a stickler for breakfast, the most important meal of the day. Babycakes comes to the rescue on many a morning.

| | Nonstick baking spray | |
| 1 to 8 | large eggs | 1 to 8 |

1. Spray wells with nonstick baking spray. Crack 1 egg into each well. Bake for 5 to 9 minutes or until eggs are cooked to desired doneness. Using a small offset spatula, carefully transfer eggs to a serving plate.

Bacon and Egg Toast Cups

These are perfect for a brunch or for enticing toddlers to enjoy a miniature version of an adult classic.

Tip
This recipe works best with fresh bread that can be rolled very thin.

Variation
Sprinkle about 1 tsp (5 mL) shredded Cheddar cheese into each cup on top of the bacon.

8	slices sandwich bread	8
2 tsp	butter, softened, or spreadable margarine	10 mL
4	slices bacon, cooked crisp and crumbled	4
1	egg	1
1/3 cup	milk	75 mL

1. Using a rolling pin, roll each slice of bread until it is very thin. Use the large circle of the crust cutting tool to cut a circle from each slice (discard scraps or reserve for another use). Spread one side of each circle with butter.

2. Place 1 bread circle, buttered side down, on top of each well and gently press into well with the pie forming tool, making a cup. Divide bacon evenly among bread cups.

3. In a small bowl, whisk together egg and milk. Spoon about 1 tbsp (15 mL) egg mixture into each bread cup.

4. Bake for 8 to 10 minutes or until a tester inserted in the center of the filling comes out clean.

Green Chile Egg Cups

**Makes
8 tortilla cups**

Green chiles add
the perfect hint of
south-of-the-border
flavor to these eggs.

Tip
Salsa verde is green salsa,
a Mexican sauce typically
made of tomatillos, green
chiles and cilantro. Look
for jars of this popular salsa
shelved with other Latin
American foods.

2	8- to 10-inch (20 to 25 cm) flour tortillas	2
1	egg	1
2 tbsp	milk	30 mL
2 tbsp	canned chopped mild green chiles	30 mL
1/4 tsp	ground cumin	1 mL
	Salt and freshly ground black pepper	
1/2 cup	shredded Monterey Jack cheese	125 mL
4 tsp	salsa verde	20 mL
	Minced fresh cilantro	

1. Working with 1 tortilla at a time, wrap tortilla in a paper towel and microwave on High for about 20 seconds or just until warm. Using the large circle of the crust cutting tool, cut 4 circles from the warm tortilla (discard scraps or reserve for another use).

2. Place 1 tortilla circle on top of each well and very gently press into well with the pie forming tool, making a cup.

3. In a small bowl, whisk together egg, milk, chiles and cumin. Season to taste with salt and pepper. Stir in cheese. Spoon about 2 tbsp (30 mL) egg mixture into each tortilla cup.

4. Bake for 9 to 10 minutes or until tortillas are crisp and a tester inserted in the center of the filling comes out clean.

5. Carefully transfer egg cups to a serving plate and garnish each with 1/2 tsp (2 mL) salsa verde. Sprinkle with cilantro.

Favorite Cheese Quiches

Makes 8 quiches

Everyday breakfast can become warm and wonderful with this easy quiche recipe.

Tips

Quiches freeze well. Place cooled quiches in an airtight container, label and freeze for up to 1 month. Let thaw overnight in the refrigerator. Place on a baking sheet and reheat in a 350°F (180°C) oven or toaster oven for 5 to 10 minutes or until hot.

A classic cheese for quiche is Gruyère, a hard, yellow Swiss cheese. However, other cheeses work just as well, on their own or in combination. You might use a mild Cheddar or Colby-Jack if serving these to children, and use a combination of Gruyère or Swiss with Romano and aged provolone for a more adult flavor. If you have several different cheeses on hand, make a variety of quiches so that everyone can have their favorite.

Variations

Substitute milk for the cream, if desired.

Add 1 tsp (5 mL) crumbled crisply cooked bacon or chopped drained roasted red bell pepper to each cup along with the cheese.

Crusts

Favorite Pie Crust (page 114) or store-bought refrigerated pie crust (see tip, page 141)

Filling

½ cup	shredded Cheddar, Swiss or other favorite cheese (see tip, at left)	125 mL
1	egg	1
⅓ cup	half-and-half (10%) cream	75 mL
	Salt and freshly ground black pepper	

1. *Crusts:* Use the large circle of the crust cutting tool to cut 8 crusts. Place crusts evenly on top of wells and gently press into wells with the pie forming tool. If desired, crimp the top edge.

2. *Filling:* Spoon 1 tbsp (15 mL) cheese into each crust.

3. In a small bowl, whisk together egg and cream. Season to taste with salt and pepper. Spoon about 1 tbsp (15 mL) egg mixture into each crust.

4. Bake for 10 to 12 minutes or until a tester inserted in the center of a quiche comes out clean and crusts are golden brown.

Cheddar, Ham and Broccoli Quiches

**Makes
8 quiches**

This favorite flavor combination in a bite-size quiche is perfect anytime and any day — from a simple family breakfast to a special holiday brunch.

Tips

If using a store-bought refrigerated pie crust, let come to room temperature, then unroll according to package directions and proceed with the recipe. If you roll the dough thin enough, you can cut 8 Babycakes two-crust pie crusts from one 14-oz (400 g) package.

You can use ½ cup (125 mL) drained thawed frozen broccoli, finely chopped, instead of fresh. In step 2, add it to the skillet with the ham.

Variations

Substitute milk for the cream, if desired.

Substitute 2 slices of bacon, cooked crisp and crumbled, for the ham. Omit the butter and cook the broccoli and onion in the bacon fat.

Crusts

	Favorite Pie Crust (page 114) or store-bought refrigerated pie crust (see tip, at left)	

Filling

1 tbsp	butter	15 mL
½ cup	finely chopped broccoli	125 mL
2 tbsp	finely chopped onion	30 mL
⅓ cup	finely chopped cooked ham	75 mL
1	egg	1
⅓ cup	half-and-half (10%) cream	75 mL
1 tsp	Dijon mustard	5 mL
⅓ cup	shredded Cheddar cheese	75 mL
	Salt and freshly ground black pepper	

1. *Crusts:* Use the large circle of the crust cutting tool to cut 8 crusts. Place crusts evenly on top of wells and gently press into wells with the pie forming tool. If desired, crimp the top edge.

2. *Filling:* In a small skillet, melt butter over medium-high heat. Sauté broccoli and onion for 3 to 5 minutes or until tender. Stir in ham and sauté for 1 minute or until heated through. Remove from heat.

3. In a medium bowl, whisk together egg, cream and mustard. Stir in cheese. Season to taste with salt and pepper. Stir in ham mixture. Spoon about 2 tbsp (30 mL) filling into each crust.

4. Bake for 10 to 12 minutes or until a tester inserted in the center of a quiche comes out clean and crusts are golden brown.

Breakfast Enchilada Cups

Make breakfast a fiesta with these enchilada cups. They're so easy to make that going through the drive-through on your way to work or school will seem like more effort!

Tips

For 2½ tbsp (37 mL) cooked pork sausage, you'll need about 1½ oz (45 g) uncooked meat, browned and drained.

Top the enchilada cups with chopped seeded tomatoes, sliced pitted ripe olives, salsa or minced fresh cilantro, if desired.

Variations

Substitute 2 slices of bacon, cooked crisp and crumbled, chopped cooked ham or cooked chorizo for the sausage.

Like spicy food? Add 4 to 5 drops of hot pepper sauce with the salsa.

2	8- to 10-inch (20 to 25 cm) flour tortillas	2
1	egg	1
2 tbsp	milk	30 mL
2 tbsp	salsa	30 mL
½ cup	shredded Cheddar or Colby-Jack cheese	125 mL
2½ tbsp	crumbled cooked pork sausage (see tip, at left)	37 mL
	Salt and freshly ground black pepper	
8 tsp	sour cream	40 mL
	Finely chopped green onion	

1. Working with 1 tortilla at a time, wrap tortilla in a paper towel and microwave on High for about 20 seconds or just until warm. Using the large circle of the crust cutting tool, cut 4 circles from the warm tortilla (discard scraps or reserve for another use).

2. Place 1 tortilla circle on top of each well and very gently press into well with the pie forming tool, making a cup.

3. In a small bowl, whisk egg, milk and salsa. Stir in cheese and sausage. Season to taste with salt and pepper. Spoon about 2 tbsp (30 mL) egg mixture into each tortilla cup.

4. Bake for 9 to 10 minutes or until tortillas are crisp and a tester inserted in the center of the filling comes out clean.

5. Carefully transfer cups to a serving plate and garnish each with 1 tsp (5 mL) sour cream. Sprinkle with green onion.

Cheesy Hash Browns

These are the perfect accompaniment at breakfast, brunch or any meal. Since they are so much easier to prepare than frying hash brown potatoes, you will serve them often.

Tip

Partially thawed hash browns may still be cold and somewhat icy, but will no longer be solidly frozen. To thaw, pour about 2½ cups (625 mL) hash browns into a bowl and let stand at room temperature for 30 minutes. By that time, any frozen clumps of hash browns should be easy to break apart, and they will measure just about 2 cups (500 mL).

2	eggs	2
2 cups	frozen shredded hash brown potatoes, partially thawed (see tip, at left)	500 mL
½ cup	shredded Cheddar cheese	125 mL
1 tbsp	all-purpose flour	15 mL
½ tsp	salt	2 mL
¼ tsp	freshly ground black pepper	1 mL
1 tbsp	butter, melted	15 mL
	Nonstick baking spray	

1. In a medium bowl, whisk eggs. Stir in hash browns, cheese, flour, salt, pepper and butter.

2. Spray wells with nonstick baking spray. Fill each well with a heaping 2 tbsp (30 mL) egg mixture. Bake for 10 to 11 minutes or until hash browns are golden brown and crisp on the sides. Using a spatula, carefully transfer hash browns to a serving plate. Repeat with the remaining egg mixture.

Favorite Breakfast Puffs

**Makes
18 puffs**

We had the pleasure
of working with
Johanna Gordy Brown
in Austin, Texas, on a
video shoot, and she
shared this wonderful
recipe with us.
Thanks, Johanna!

1½ cups	all-purpose flour	375 mL
1½ tsp	baking powder	7 mL
½ tsp	salt	2 mL
¼ tsp	ground nutmeg	1 mL
1 cup	granulated sugar, divided	250 mL
⅓ cup	shortening	75 mL
1	egg	1
½ cup	milk	125 mL
1 tsp	ground cinnamon	5 mL
6 tbsp	butter, melted	90 mL

1. In a small bowl, whisk together flour, baking powder, salt and nutmeg. Set aside.

2. In a large bowl, using an electric mixer on medium-high speed, beat together ½ cup (125 mL) of the sugar and shortening for 1 to 2 minutes or until fluffy. Beat in egg. Add flour mixture alternately with milk, making three additions of flour and two of milk and beating on low speed until smooth.

3. Fill each well with about 1½ tbsp (22 mL) batter (do not use paper liners). Bake for 6 to 8 minutes or until a tester inserted in the center of a puff comes out clean.

4. Meanwhile, in a small bowl, combine the remaining sugar and cinnamon.

5. Transfer hot puffs to a serving plate and immediately roll in melted butter, then in cinnamon-sugar. Repeat with the remaining batter, rolling each batch in butter then cinnamon-sugar as they are baked.

Lemon Meringue Mini Pies (page 124)

Rustic Apple Strudel Tarts (page 134)

Cheddar, Ham and Broccoli Quiches (page 141)

Curried Chicken Salad Cups (page 152)

Ham and Cheese'wiches (page 166)

Brownie Tarts (page 180)

Empanadas with Pork and Caper Filling (page 192)

Easter Basket Cupcakes
(page 198)

White Chocolate Snowmen Cupcakes (page 206)

Southern-Style Biscuits

**Makes
12 to 13 biscuits**

Whether you make
them for breakfast,
for brunch or as an
appetizer with a savory
filling, these bite-size
biscuits will become
one of your favorite
recipes.

Tip

No buttermilk on hand?
Stir 1½ tsp (7 mL) lemon
juice or white vinegar into
½ cup (125 mL) milk. Let
stand for 5 to 10 minutes
or until thickened. Proceed
with the recipe.

Variation

Make Southern-style
appetizers by cutting
biscuits in half horizontally
and layering them with
small pieces of country ham
and cheese.

• 2-inch (5 cm) round cookie cutter

2 cups	all-purpose flour	500 mL
2 tsp	baking powder	10 mL
¼ tsp	baking soda	1 mL
¼ tsp	salt	1 mL
1 tbsp	butter	15 mL
1 tbsp	shortening	15 mL
½ cup	buttermilk (see tip, at left)	125 mL

1. In a medium bowl, whisk together flour, baking powder, baking soda and salt. Using your fingertips or a pastry blender, blend in butter and shortening until mixture is coarse and crumbly. Using a fork, stir in buttermilk just until dough comes together (it will be very sticky).

2. Turn dough out onto a floured surface and gently knead 4 or 5 times. Pat into a ¾-inch (2 cm) thick circle. Using the cookie cutter, cut out 12 or 13 biscuits, rerolling scraps as necessary.

3. Place a biscuit in each well. Bake for 5 minutes. Carefully turn biscuits over and bake for 5 to 6 minutes or until golden brown on top. Transfer hot biscuits to a serving plate. Repeat with the remaining dough.

Scones

**Makes
8 scones**

When you can't be
at the Ritz-Carlton
enjoying afternoon
tea, these scones are
the next best thing.
Serve with jam and
clotted cream.

Tip

For tender, flaky scones,
keep the butter and
whipping cream very cold
and do not overwork the
dough.

Variation

Knead in 1½ tbsp (22 mL)
dried currants in step 3.

• 2-inch (5 cm) round cookie cutter

1 cup	all-purpose flour	250 mL
2 tbsp	granulated sugar	30 mL
1 tsp	baking powder	5 mL
Pinch	salt	Pinch
3 tbsp	cold butter, cut into small pieces	45 mL
1	egg yolk	1
¼ cup	heavy or whipping (35%) cream	60 mL
½ tsp	vanilla extract	2 mL

1. In a medium bowl, whisk together flour, sugar, baking powder and salt. Using your fingertips or a pastry blender, blend in butter until mixture is coarse and crumbly.

2. In a small bowl, whisk together egg yolk, cream and vanilla. Add to flour mixture and, using a fork, stir until just combined (do not overmix).

3. Turn dough out onto a floured surface and gently knead 4 or 5 times. Pat into a ¾-inch (2 cm) thick circle. Using the cookie cutter, cut out 8 scones, rerolling scraps as necessary.

4. Place a scone in each well. Bake for 5 minutes. Carefully turn scones over and bake for 5 to 6 minutes or until light brown.

Mini Caramel Pecan Sticky Buns

Makes 11 buns

These warm cinnamon rolls, dripping with warm caramel and pecans, are over-the-top spectacular.

Tips

Toasting pecans intensifies their flavor. Spread chopped pecans in a single layer on a baking sheet. Bake at 350°F (180°C) for 5 to 7 minutes or until lightly browned. Let cool, then measure.

Spray the wells with nonstick baking spray in between batches for easy cleanup.

When you're done baking, wet a paper towel and carefully wipe out the wells before the machine has cooled completely and the sugars have hardened.

Buns

1	can (8 oz/227 g) refrigerated crescent roll dough	1
¼ cup	granulated sugar	60 mL
½ tsp	ground cinnamon	2 mL
	Nonstick baking spray	

Topping

1 tbsp	butter	15 mL
¼ cup	packed brown sugar	60 mL
2 tbsp	heavy or whipping (35%) cream	30 mL
⅓ cup	chopped pecans, toasted (see tip, at left)	75 mL
½ tsp	vanilla extract	2 mL

1. *Buns:* Carefully unroll dough, keeping it in one piece. Press seams together to make an 11- by 8-inch (28 by 20 cm) rectangle. Set aside.

2. In a small bowl, whisk together sugar and cinnamon. Sprinkle evenly over dough. Starting from a long end, roll up dough like a jelly roll. Pinch seam to seal. Slice roll into 11 spirals, each about 1 inch (2.5 cm) thick.

3. Spray wells with nonstick baking spray. Place 1 spiral in each well and bake for 3 to 4 minutes or until bottoms are golden brown. Using a small offset spatula, carefully turn buns over and bake for 3 minutes or until golden brown and a tester inserted in the center of dough comes out clean. Transfer buns to a wire rack to cool slightly. Carefully wipe out wells with a wet paper towel. Repeat with the remaining batter.

4. *Topping:* Place butter in a microwave-safe glass bowl. Microwave on High for 30 to 40 seconds or until melted. Stir in brown sugar and microwave on High for 30 seconds. Stir well. Microwave on High for about 10 seconds or until sugar is melted and mixture is bubbling. Stir in cream until well blended. Microwave on High for about 10 seconds or until bubbling. Stir until smooth. Stir in pecans and vanilla.

5. Arrange buns side by side on a deep serving platter. Spoon topping over warm buns.

Cinni Minis

There's no need to rush to the bakery on Saturday mornings to purchase treats for your family. Now you can make warm miniature cinnamon rolls in minutes.

Tips

Spray the wells with nonstick baking spray in between batches for easy cleanup.

When you're done baking, wet a paper towel and carefully wipe out the wells before the machine has cooled completely and the sugars have hardened.

Rolls

1	can (8 oz/227 g) refrigerated crescent roll dough	1
¼ cup	granulated sugar	60 mL
½ tsp	ground cinnamon	2 mL
	Nonstick baking spray	

Glaze

3 tbsp	confectioners' (icing) sugar	45 mL
¼ tsp	vanilla extract	1 mL
1 to 3 tsp	milk	5 to 15 mL

1. *Rolls:* Carefully unroll dough, keeping it in one piece. Press seams together to make an 11- by 8-inch (28 by 20 cm) rectangle. Set aside.

2. In a small bowl, whisk together sugar and cinnamon. Sprinkle evenly over dough. Starting from a long end, roll up dough like a jelly roll. Pinch seam to seal. Slice roll into 11 spirals, each about 1 inch (2.5 cm) thick.

3. Spray wells with nonstick baking spray. Place 1 spiral in each well and bake for 3 to 4 minutes or until bottoms are golden brown. Using a small offset spatula, carefully turn rolls over and bake for 3 minutes or until golden brown and a tester inserted in the center of dough comes out clean. Transfer rolls to a wire rack to cool slightly. Carefully wipe out wells with a wet paper towel. Repeat with the remaining spirals.

4. *Glaze:* In a small bowl, whisk together confectioners' sugar and vanilla. Whisk in milk, 1 tsp (5 mL) at a time, until the mixture has the consistency of glaze. Drizzle over warm rolls.

Lunch and Supper

Garlic Toast Bites

**Makes
8 toast cups**

Now there's no need
to buy an entire loaf of
Italian bread for a tasty
accompaniment to an
Italian meal.

Tip

You may find it easier to push
the bread circles into the wells
using your fingers, especially
if the bread is fresh. But only
do this if you're beginning
with a cold appliance; use
the pie forming tool if the
appliance is hot.

8	slices white bread	8
1/2 tsp	garlic salt	2 mL
2 tbsp	olive oil	30 mL
8 tsp	freshly grated Parmesan cheese	40 mL

1. Use the small circle of the crust cutting tool to cut a circle from each bread slice (discard scraps or reserve for another use). Place 1 bread circle on top of each well and gently press into well with the pie forming tool, making a cup.

2. In a small bowl, combine garlic salt and oil. Brush evenly over bread cups.

3. Bake for 6 to 8 minutes or until bread cups are lightly toasted and crisp. Sprinkle each cup with 1 tsp (5 mL) Parmesan. Bake for 30 seconds or until cheese is melted. Serve warm.

Jalapeño Cheese Biscuits

**Makes
14 to 16 biscuits**

Add some spice to
your biscuits. These
easy biscuits taste great
alongside chili or salad,
or filled as an appetizer.

Tip

If three-cheese biscuit mix
isn't available, substitute
1¾ cups (425 mL) regular
biscuit mix (such as Bisquick)
and add ¼ cup (60 mL)
shredded Cheddar cheese
and 2 tbsp (30 mL) freshly
grated Parmesan cheese.

• **2-inch (5 cm) round cookie cutter**

1	package (7¾ oz/219 g) three-cheese biscuit mix, such as Bisquick Complete	1
1 to 2 tbsp	drained chopped pickled jalapeño peppers	15 to 30 mL
1/2 cup	water	125 mL

1. In a medium bowl, using a fork, stir together biscuit mix, jalapeños to taste and water just until blended.

2. Turn dough out onto a floured surface and gently knead 4 or 5 times. Pat into a ¾-inch (2 cm) thick circle. Using the cookie cutter, cut out 14 to 16 biscuits, rerolling scraps as necessary.

3. Place a biscuit into each well. Bake for 3 minutes. Carefully turn biscuits over and bake for 3 to 5 minutes or until golden brown on top. Transfer hot biscuits to a serving plate. Repeat with the remaining dough. Serve warm.

Shrimp Sauté in Crisp Pita Cups

Makes 8 pita cups

This dish comes together at lightning speed, and the flavor matches any from a gourmet restaurant.

Tips

Choose fresh, soft, thin pita breads for these cups. Pita breads that are dry or thicker may tear more easily when pressed into the wells.

Keep a package of deveined peeled shrimp in the freezer for this recipe. You only need to thaw the shrimp slightly — just enough so you can easily chop them.

Variations

Try serving these in Wonton Cups (page 120) instead of pita cups.

For an attractive presentation, prepare the recipe as directed and fill cups. Then cook 8 small or medium shrimp, peeled and deveined, in a little olive oil until pink and opaque. If desired, season with salt, lemon pepper and lemon juice. Using a slotted spoon, lift shrimp from juices and place 1 shrimp on top of each filled cup. Garnish each with a parsley leaf.

Crusts

2	6-inch (15 cm) pita pockets (see tip, at left)	2
	Nonstick baking spray	

Filling

1 tsp	olive oil	5 mL
2	cloves garlic, minced	2
⅔ cup	chopped deveined peeled shrimp, partially thawed if frozen (about 5 oz/150 g)	150 mL
2 tsp	capers, rinsed and drained	10 mL
½ tsp	ground lemon pepper	2 mL
¼ tsp	salt	1 mL
2 tsp	freshly squeezed lemon juice	10 mL
2 tsp	minced fresh flat-leaf (Italian) parsley	10 mL
8	fresh flat-leaf (Italian) parsley leaves	8

1. *Crusts:* Using kitchen shears, cut outside edge from each pita and separate into two thin rounds. Wrap rounds in a paper towel and microwave on High for 20 seconds or just until warm.

2. Using the small circle of the crust cutting tool, imprint 2 circles on each round. Using kitchen shears, cut out circles. Place a circle on top of each well and gently press into well with the pie forming tool, making a cup. Spray cups with nonstick baking spray.

3. Bake for 5 to 6 minutes or until pita cups are crisp. Carefully transfer to a wire rack to cool slightly.

4. *Filling:* Meanwhile, in a small skillet, heat oil over medium-high heat. Sauté garlic for 30 seconds or until fragrant. Add shrimp, capers, lemon pepper and salt; sauté for 2 to 3 minutes or until shrimp begin to turn pink. Add lemon juice and cook, stirring, for 1 minute or until shrimp are pink and opaque. Stir in minced parsley.

5. Using a slotted spoon, spoon about 1 tbsp (15 mL) shrimp mixture into each pita cup. Garnish with a parsley leaf. Serve immediately.

Curried Chicken Salad Cups

Gingerroot and curry add a bit of the exotic to the usual chicken salad. Although they are ideal for lunch and supper, they also make impressive appetizers for your next book club, dinner party or potluck.

Tip

We like to leave the wonton wrappers whole (square) for this recipe, so that the filled cup has rustic, browned edges. If you prefer smoother edges, follow the directions on page 120 and cut the wonton wrappers into circles before filling.

Crusts

16	wonton wrappers (about 3½ inches/ 8.5 cm square)	16

Filling

1	clove garlic, minced	1
1 tsp	grated gingerroot	5 mL
½ tsp	curry powder	2 mL
3 tbsp	whipped cream cheese, softened	45 mL
3 tbsp	sour cream	45 mL
1 tsp	freshly squeezed lemon juice	5 mL
1	green onion, chopped	1
1 cup	chopped cooked chicken	250 mL
3 tbsp	sweetened dried cranberries or golden raisins	45 mL
2 tbsp	dry-roasted peanuts	30 mL
	Salt and freshly ground black pepper	

Garnish

Additional dry-roasted peanuts (optional)
Minced fresh cilantro

1. *Crusts:* Place 1 wonton wrapper on top of each well and gently press into well with the pie forming tool, making a cup.

2. *Filling:* In a medium bowl, combine garlic, ginger, curry powder, cream cheese, sour cream and lemon juice. Stir in green onion, chicken, cranberries and peanuts. Season to taste with salt and pepper. Spoon about 1½ tbsp (22 mL) filling into each wonton cup.

3. Bake for 6 to 8 minutes or until wontons are golden and filling is hot. Carefully transfer cups to a wire rack to cool slightly. Repeat with the remaining wontons and filling.

4. *Garnish:* Sprinkle with additional peanuts (if using) and cilantro. Serve immediately.

Chicken and Green Chile Hand Pies

**Makes
8 hand pies**

These little pies remind
us of a great trip we
took to Albuquerque,
New Mexico, where we
had the opportunity
to study chiles and
Southwestern food. The
trip was particularly
special for us because
our husbands went
with us and shared
in all the fun!

Variations

Substitute shredded
Cheddar or Monterey Jack
cheese for the cheese
blend.

Want a bit more heat? Add
3 to 5 drops of hot pepper
sauce to the filling.

Replace the chopped
cooked chicken with 1 can
(4½ oz/128 g) chicken,
drained.

Crusts

	Favorite Pie Crust (page 114) or store-bought refrigerated pie crust (see tip, page 141)	

Filling

½ cup	chopped cooked chicken	125 mL
½ cup	shredded Mexican cheese blend	125 mL
1 tbsp	canned chopped mild green chiles	15 mL
½ tsp	ground cumin	2 mL
	Salt and freshly ground black pepper	
1	egg	1
1 tbsp	water	15 mL

1. *Crusts:* Use the large circle of the crust cutting tool to cut 8 bottom crusts, and use the small circle to cut 8 top crusts, rerolling scraps as necessary. Place large crusts evenly on top of wells and gently press into wells with the pie forming tool.

2. *Filling:* In a small bowl, combine chicken, cheese, chiles and cumin. Season to taste with salt and pepper.

3. Spoon about 1½ tbsp (22 mL) filling into each bottom crust. Place small crusts directly over the center of each filled shell.

4. In a small bowl, whisk together egg and water. Brush lightly over top crusts.

5. Bake for 12 to 15 minutes or until crusts are browned and crisp. Serve immediately.

BLT Cups

**Makes
8 toast cups**

What a fun twist on a classic sandwich! And it's ready for lunch or supper in minutes.

Tips

For this recipe, make the Toast Cups using the small circle of the crust cutting tool.

To save even more time, you can use 2 tbsp (30 mL) real bacon bits instead of the crumbled bacon.

Quarter 4 grape or small cherry tomatoes and use them as garnish in place of the tomato pieces.

4 tsp	mayonnaise	20 mL
8	small Toast Cups (page 118)	8
2	slices bacon, cooked crisp and crumbled	2
½ cup	finely shredded lettuce	125 mL
1	small ripe tomato, seeded and cut into ¼-inch (0.5 cm) pieces	1

1. Spoon about ½ tsp (2 mL) mayonnaise into each toast cup. Top with about ¾ tsp (3 mL) bacon, then with 1 tbsp (15 mL) shredded lettuce. Garnish with tomato. Serve immediately.

Bacon and Cheese Crostini Cups

Is it a hot sandwich or a rich appetizer? You decide. Either way, it's scrumptious.

Variation
Replace the white bread with any soft fresh bread, such as whole wheat or sourdough.

8	slices white bread	8
3	slices bacon, cooked crisp and crumbled	3
1	small green onion, chopped	1
½ cup	shredded Monterey Jack cheese	125 mL
⅛ tsp	garlic powder	0.5 mL
3 tbsp	mayonnaise	45 mL
Dash	hot pepper sauce	Dash
	Salt and freshly ground black pepper	

1. Using a rolling pin, roll each slice of bread until it is very thin. Use the large circle of the crust cutting tool to cut a circle from each slice (discard scraps or reserve for another use).

2. Place 1 bread circle on top of each well and gently press into well with the pie forming tool, making a cup.

3. In a medium bowl, combine bacon, green onion, cheese, garlic powder, mayonnaise and hot pepper sauce. Season to taste with salt and pepper. Spoon 1 to 1½ tbsp (15 to 22 mL) bacon mixture into each bread cup.

4. Bake for 6 to 8 minutes or until filling is hot, cheese is melted and cups are golden brown and crisp. Serve immediately.

Italian Sausage Pizza Bites

Capture the flavor of
your favorite pizza in
these little bites —
perfect for lunch
or supper, or as an
appetizer.

Tips

Purchase bulk Italian
sausage or remove meat
from casings before
cooking.

Garnish these pizza
bites with your choice of
toppings. We like sliced
pitted ripe olives, sliced
fresh basil and thinly sliced
roasted red bell pepper.

Variation

Substitute ground beef or
any flavor of pork sausage
for the Italian sausage.
Add 2 tbsp (30 mL) finely
chopped onion when
browning the meat, and
season with $\frac{1}{2}$ to 1 tsp
(2 to 5 mL) dry Italian herb
seasoning.

8	Pizza Crusts (page 116), prepared through step 3	8
4 oz	Italian sausage (see tip, at left)	125 g
$\frac{1}{4}$ cup	pizza sauce	60 mL
$\frac{1}{4}$ tsp	dried oregano	1 mL
4 tsp	shredded mozzarella cheese	20 mL
4 tsp	freshly grated Parmesan cheese	20 mL
	Toppings as desired (see tip, at left)	

1. In a small skillet, cook sausage over medium-high heat, breaking it up with the back of a spoon, for 6 to 8 minutes or until no longer pink. Remove from heat and drain off fat. Stir in pizza sauce and oregano.

2. Meanwhile, bake pizza crusts for 7 minutes or until crust is set and beginning to dry.

3. Spoon about $\frac{1}{2}$ tsp (2 mL) mozzarella into each partially baked pizza cup. Top with 1 tbsp (15 mL) sausage mixture.

4. Bake for 5 to 7 minutes or until filling is hot and crusts are crisp. Transfer pizza bites to a wire rack to cool slightly.

5. Sprinkle pizza bites with Parmesan, then garnish with toppings as desired. Serve warm.

Mexican Tortilla Cups

**Makes
8 tortilla cups**

When you want a quick hot lunch that makes a nice change from a sandwich, these Mexican cups will hit the spot.

....

Tips

For the toppings, try sour cream, guacamole, sliced pickled jalapeño peppers, sliced pitted ripe olives and/ or sliced green onions.

For a change of pace, try a corn and black bean salsa — or any other salsa — instead of the usual tomato salsa.

Variation

Substitute $1/4$ cup (60 mL) cooked taco meat or cooked or canned chili for the refried beans.

2	8- to 10-inch (20 to 25 cm) flour tortillas	2
$1/4$ cup	refried beans	60 mL
$1/2$ cup	shredded Mexican cheese blend	125 mL
3 to 4 tbsp	salsa	45 to 60 mL

Toppings as desired (see tip, at left)

1. Working with 1 tortilla at a time, wrap tortilla in a paper towel and microwave on High for about 20 seconds or just until warm. Using the large circle of the crust cutting tool, cut 4 circles from the warm tortilla (discard scraps or reserve for another use).

2. Place 1 tortilla circle on top of each well and very gently press into well with the pie forming tool, making a cup.

3. Spoon about $1\frac{1}{2}$ tsp (7 mL) refried beans into each tortilla cup. Top with about 1 tbsp (15 mL) cheese, then with 1 to $1\frac{1}{2}$ tsp (5 to 7 mL) salsa.

4. Bake for 5 to 6 minutes or until tortillas are crisp and filling is hot. Transfer cups to a wire rack to cool slightly.

5. Garnish tortilla cups with toppings as desired. Serve warm.

Lunch and Supper   **157**

Individual Meat and Veggie Pot Pies

Makes 8 hand pies

Are there odds and ends left over in your refrigerator? No problem! Plan on pot pies for lunch or supper. Homemade pot pies taste so much better than the frozen variety. Use your favorite combinations of meat and vegetables for a comforting meal.

Tips

The possibilities for these pot pies are endless. Try combining roast beef, potatoes and brown gravy; chicken, peas, carrots or mushrooms and chicken gravy; or pork roast, corn and brown gravy.

Use only fully cooked meat and vegetables in these pot pies. If you don't have leftovers, stop by the deli counter and purchase cooked meat and vegetables.

Variation

Only have leftover veggies? No problem. Just replace the meat with another ½ cup (125 mL) chopped cooked vegetables.

Crusts

	Favorite Pie Crust (page 114) or store-bought refrigerated pie crust (see tip, page 141)	

Filling

½ cup	chopped cooked chicken, beef or pork	125 mL
½ cup	chopped cooked vegetables (such as potatoes, carrots, onions or a combination)	125 mL
¼ tsp	dried thyme, rosemary or tarragon	1 mL
¼ cup	prepared chicken or brown gravy	60 mL
	Salt and freshly ground black pepper	
1	egg	1
1 tbsp	water	15 mL

1. *Crusts:* Use the large circle of the crust cutting tool to cut 8 bottom crusts, and use the small circle to cut 8 top crusts, rerolling scraps as necessary. Place large crusts evenly on top of wells and gently press into wells with the pie forming tool.

2. *Filling:* In a medium bowl, combine chicken, vegetables, thyme and gravy. Season to taste with salt and pepper.

3. Spoon about 1½ tbsp (22 mL) filling into each bottom crust. Place small crusts directly over the center of each filled shell.

4. In a small bowl, whisk together egg and water. Brush lightly over top crusts.

5. Bake for 12 to 15 minutes or until crusts are browned and crisp. Serve immediately.

After-School Snacks

Pimento Cheese Cups

You don't have to be born and raised in the South to appreciate tasty pimento cheese. The combination of the toasted bread cups and the creamy cheese filling make these a wonderful snack — or even a light lunch.

Tip

The pimento cheese filling also makes an excellent vegetable dip.

6	slices white bread	6
1 tbsp	butter, softened, or spreadable margarine	15 mL
1	jar (2 oz/60 g) pimentos, drained	1
3 oz	cream cheese, softened	90 g
1 cup	shredded Cheddar cheese	250 mL
¼ cup	mayonnaise	60 mL
Pinch	garlic powder	Pinch
	Salt and freshly ground black pepper	

1. Using a rolling pin, roll each slice of bread until it is very thin. Use the small circle of the crust cutting tool to cut 2 circles from each slice, avoiding the crusts (discard scraps or reserve for another use). Spread one side of each circle with butter.

2. Place 1 bread circle, buttered side down, on top of each well and gently press into well with the pie forming tool, making a cup.

3. Bake for 6 to 8 minutes or until cups are crisp and golden brown. Transfer cups to a wire rack to cool slightly. Repeat with the remaining bread circles.

4. Set 12 pieces of pimento aside for garnish. In a medium bowl, using an electric mixer on medium speed, beat cream cheese until fluffy. Beat in the remaining pimentos, Cheddar cheese, mayonnaise, garlic powder and salt and pepper to taste until well blended.

5. Divide cheese mixture evenly among toast cups. Garnish each with 1 piece of reserved pimento. Serve immediately.

Cheese Poppers

• •

**Makes
8 mini sandwiches**

Tiny, but all fun!
These little cheese
sandwiches will hit
the spot after school.

•••••••••••••••••••••••••

Variation
Substitute any kind of
cheese you like. Provolone
and Swiss also work well.

• 1½-inch (4 cm) cookie cutter

4	slices white or whole wheat bread	4
2 tsp	butter, softened, or spreadable margarine	10 mL
2	slices (about 3¼ inches/8 cm square) American or Cheddar cheese	2

1. Using cookie cutter, cut 16 circles from each slice of bread, avoiding crusts (discard scraps or reserve for another use). Lightly spread one side of each circle with butter. Place 1 bread circle, buttered side down, in each cupcake well.

2. Using the same cookie cutter, cut 8 circles of cheese. Place 1 cheese circle on each bread circle. Top with the remaining bread circle, buttered side up.

3. Bake for 3 to 4 minutes or until bottom bread circle is toasted. Using the tip of a small offset spatula, carefully turn sandwiches over so toasted side is up. Bake for 2 to 3 minutes or until bottom is toasted and cheese is melted. Carefully transfer sandwiches to a serving plate. Serve immediately.

Taco Cups

These colorful
Mexican-inspired
morsels are great after
school or anytime!
We like to nibble on
them while we're
watching the big
game on TV. Serve
with salsa, guacamole
and sour cream.

Variation

Omit the ground beef
and substitute one 16-oz
(454 mL) can of refried
beans. Heat beans in skillet
over medium heat, then
proceed with step 2.

1 lb	lean ground beef	500 g
1 tbsp	chili powder	15 mL
1 tbsp	paprika	15 mL
1 tsp	ground cumin	5 mL
½ tsp	garlic powder	2 mL
	Salt and freshly ground black pepper	
½ cup	water	125 mL
28	baked Tortilla Cups (page 120)	28
1 cup	shredded Cheddar cheese	250 mL
1 cup	shredded lettuce	250 mL
2	plum (Roma) tomatoes, diced	2

1. In a large nonstick skillet, cook beef over medium-high heat, breaking it up with the back of a wooden spoon, for 8 to 10 minutes or until no longer pink. Drain off fat.

2. Stir in chili powder, paprika, cumin, garlic powder and salt and pepper to taste. Add water, reduce heat and simmer, stirring occasionally, for 10 minutes or until slightly thickened.

3. Divide beef mixture evenly among tortilla cups. Sprinkle evenly with cheese, lettuce and tomatoes. Serve immediately.

Nacho Cups

· ·

When it is snack time, these quick and easy nachos will hit the spot.

· ·

Tips

For the toppings, try sliced pickled jalapeños, guacamole, sour cream and minced fresh cilantro.

If you prefer a slightly smaller tortilla cup, use the small circle of the crust cutting tool to make your crusts.

2	8- to 10-inch (20 to 25 cm) flour tortillas	2
8 tsp	shredded Cheddar or Colby-Jack cheese or Mexican cheese blend	40 mL
8 tsp	salsa	40 mL
	Toppings as desired (see tip, at left)	

1. Working with 1 tortilla at a time, wrap tortilla in a paper towel and microwave on High for about 20 seconds or just until warm. Using the large circle of the crust cutting tool, cut 4 circles from the warm tortilla (discard scraps or reserve for another use).

2. Place 1 tortilla circle on top of each well and very gently press into well with the pie forming tool, making a cup. Bake for 4 minutes or until cups are hot and lightly toasted.

3. Divide cheese evenly among tortilla cups. Top with salsa.

4. Bake for 1 to 2 minutes or until cups are crisp and cheese is melted. Carefully transfer cups to a serving plate.

5. Garnish tortilla cups with toppings as desired.

Pepperoni Pizza Bites

4	slices white bread	4
8	slices pepperoni, cut into quarters	8
8 tsp	shredded mozzarella cheese	40 mL
1/4 cup	pizza sauce	60 mL
8 tsp	freshly grated Parmesan cheese	40 mL

Are you craving pizza but don't want a whole pie? These pizza bites are the answer. Let each snacker choose his or her own toppings — for example, sliced pitted ripe olives or cooked ground beef are good choices in place of the pepperoni.

Tips

If you prefer a slightly larger toast cup, use 8 slices of bread and use the large circle of the crust cutting tool to cut a circle from each slice.

If you love pepperoni, feel free to use twice as much!

If you substitute other pizza toppings, choose meats or vegetables that are fully cooked, or add those that don't require cooking, such as olives, drained canned mushrooms or minced fresh herbs, such as basil or oregano.

1. Using a rolling pin, roll each slice of bread until it is very thin. Use the small circle of the crust cutting tool to cut 2 circles from each slice, avoiding the crusts (discard scraps or reserve for another use).

2. Place 1 bread circle on top of each well and gently press into well with the pie forming tool, making a cup.

3. Divide pepperoni pieces evenly among bread cups. Sprinkle with mozzarella, then drizzle with pizza sauce.

4. Bake for 6 to 8 minutes or until cups are crisp and golden brown. Carefully transfer cups to a serving platter and sprinkle with Parmesan. Serve immediately.

Corn Dogs

There's no need to wait until the next fair or festival to indulge in a corn dog. These are great for an effortless snack (or even a speedy supper).

Tips

These are especially good served with mustard.

Paper liners are a must for this recipe, to protect your fingers from burning.

● Paper liners

¼ cup	cornmeal	60 mL
¼ cup	all-purpose flour	60 mL
1½ tsp	granulated sugar	7 mL
¾ tsp	baking powder	3 mL
¼ tsp	salt	1 mL
Pinch	cayenne pepper	Pinch
1	egg	1
2 tbsp	milk	30 mL
1 tbsp	vegetable oil	15 mL
2	frankfurters (about 4½ inches/ 11 cm long), each cut into 12 slices (or 8 cooked cocktail sausages, cut into thirds)	2

1. In a medium bowl, whisk together cornmeal, flour, sugar, baking powder, salt and cayenne. Set aside.

2. In a small bowl, whisk together egg, milk and oil. Pour over cornmeal mixture and stir until blended.

3. Place paper liners in wells. Place 3 frankfurter slices (or 3 cocktail sausage thirds) in each well. Spoon batter over frankfurters, dividing evenly.

4. Bake for 5 to 7 minutes or until a tester inserted into the center of a corn dog comes out clean. Serve warm.

Ham and Cheese'wiches

**Makes
8 toast cups**

Are you tired of the same old cold deli sandwiches and overly filling panini? Bite-size open-face sandwiches are a sure way to beat the blahs.

Variation

Substitute thinly sliced deli turkey or roast beef for the ham.

8	slices white or whole wheat bread	8
2 tsp	butter, softened, or spreadable margarine	10 mL
4	thin slices deli ham, cut into small pieces	4
8 tsp	shredded Cheddar cheese	40 mL

1. Using a rolling pin, roll each slice of bread until it is very thin. Use the large circle of the crust cutting tool to cut a circle from each slice (discard scraps or reserve for another use). Spread one side of each circle with butter.

2. Place 1 bread circle, buttered side down, on top of each well and gently press into well with the pie forming tool, making a cup.

3. Divide ham evenly among bread cups. Sprinkle evenly with cheese.

4. Bake for 6 to 8 minutes or until cheese is melted and cups are crisp and golden brown.

Peanut Butter and Jelly Cups

**Makes
8 cookie cups**

Kids of all ages love peanut butter and jelly, and these scrumptious bites sweeten the mix, yet keep it quick and easy. As the cookie dough bakes and then cools, it becomes slightly cupped — the perfect shape for a jam filling!

Tips

Wrap leftover dough tightly in plastic wrap and refrigerate for up to 1 day or freeze for up to 9 months. Let dough partially thaw in the refrigerator, then slice and proceed with the recipe or use as desired in another recipe.

Paper liners are a must for this recipe, to protect your fingers from burning.

Be sure to let the cookie cups cool completely before filling and serving.

Variations

Use your favorite kind of jam or jelly in these sweet cups.

Peanut Butter and Chocolate Cups: Omit the jam. After transferring the cookies to a wire rack, immediately spoon about $\frac{1}{2}$ tsp (2 mL) mini chocolate chips onto each hot cookie. Let cool before serving.

• Paper liners

5$\frac{1}{2}$ oz	refrigerated peanut butter cookie dough (about $\frac{1}{3}$ of a 16$\frac{1}{2}$-oz/ 468 g roll)	156 g
4 tsp	strawberry jam	20 mL

1. Slice cookie dough into 4 equal slices, about $\frac{1}{2}$ inch (1 cm) wide. Cut each slice in half and shape into a rounded, flat disk about 1$\frac{1}{2}$ inches (4 cm) in diameter.

2. Place paper liners in wells. Place 1 dough disk in each well.

3. Bake for 11 to 13 minutes or until cookies are golden brown and edges are crisp. (Cookies will be soft and will harden as they cool.) Using a small offset spatula, carefully transfer cookies to a wire rack to cool completely.

4. Spoon jam into the center of each cookie cup, dividing equally.

Cinnamon Toast Cups

The aroma of these quick and easy cups will lure everyone to the kitchen. They're a great snack anytime you want a pick-me-up.

Tip
Use a small offset spatula to lift the toast cups from the wells. Be careful not to scrape the coating on the cupcake maker.

4	slices white bread	4
2 tbsp	butter, melted	30 mL
1 tbsp	granulated sugar	15 mL
½ tsp	ground cinnamon	2 mL

1. Use the small circle of the crust cutting tool to cut 2 circles from each slice of bread, avoiding the crusts (discard scraps or reserve for another use).

2. Place 1 bread circle, buttered side down, on top of each well and gently press into well with the pie forming tool, making a cup. Brush the inside of each cup with butter.

3. In a small bowl, combine sugar and cinnamon. Sprinkle evenly inside each bread cup.

4. Bake for 6 to 8 minutes or until cups are crisp and golden brown. Using a small offset spatula, carefully transfer cups to a wire rack to cool slightly. Serve warm.

Vanilla Wafer S'mores

• •

Makes 8 s'mores

Some days, warm, oozing chocolate and melted marshmallows are just what the doctor ordered.

• •

Tip

Don't serve s'mores immediately after baking — they are just too hot — but be sure to serve them while they're still warm.

Paper liners are a must for this recipe, to protect your fingers from burning.

Variations

Substitute milk chocolate chips, peanut butter chips or butterscotch chips for the semisweet chocolate chips.

Spoon ½ tsp (2 mL) chocolate hazelnut spread or peanut butter over the flat side of each cookie before adding the marshmallows and chocolate chips.

• Paper liners

16	vanilla wafer cookies, divided	16
24	mini marshmallows (about ¼ cup/60 mL)	24
3 to 4 tbsp	semisweet chocolate chips	45 to 60 mL

1. Place paper liners in wells. Place 1 cookie, flat side up, in each well. Top each cookie with 3 marshmallows and 1 to 1½ tsp (5 to 7 mL) chocolate chips. Place the remaining cookies, flat side down, on top.

2. Bake for 4 to 5 minutes or until chocolate and marshmallows are melted. Carefully transfer s'mores to a wire rack to cool slightly. Serve warm.

Chocolate Candy Crunch Brownie Bites

Make these brownie bites on the weekend, and you will have after-school snacks (or lunch box treats) ready all week.

Tips

Paper liners are a must for this recipe, to protect your fingers from burning.

Be sure to let brownie bites cool completely before serving.

Store cooled brownie bites in an airtight container at room temperature for up to 4 days.

• Paper liners		
1	package (about 18 oz/550 g) brownie mix	1
	Ingredients listed on brownie package for cake-like brownies	
1 cup	candy-coated chocolate candies, coarsely crushed or chopped, divided	250 mL
	Chocolate Drizzle (page 92)	

1. Prepare brownie batter as directed on package. Stir in $1/2$ cup (125 mL) of the candies.

2. Place paper liners in wells. Fill each well with about $1\frac{1}{2}$ tbsp (22 mL) batter. Bake for 11 to 12 minutes or until set. Using a small offset spatula, carefully transfer brownie bites to a wire rack to cool completely. Repeat with the remaining batter.

3. Drizzle each brownie bite with Chocolate Drizzle. Sprinkle with the remaining candies.

Gluten-Free Favorites

Mexican Chocolate Cupcakes

**Makes
30 to 32 cupcakes**

These wonderful cupcakes feature a little hint of Mexico, as they are flavored with cinnamon and coffee. They are great frosted with Chocolate Coffee Icing (page 91) or Buttercream Frosting (page 80).

Tips

If you have a package of cake mix larger or smaller than 15 oz (425 g), measure out 2⅓ cups (575 mL).

No buttermilk on hand? Stir 1½ tsp (7 mL) lemon juice or white vinegar into ½ cup (125 mL) milk. Let stand for 5 to 10 minutes or until thickened. Proceed with the recipe.

- Paper liners (optional)

⅔ cup	sweetened applesauce	150 mL
½ cup	butter, softened	125 mL
1	package (15 oz/425 g) gluten-free devil's food cake mix	1
½ tsp	ground cinnamon	2 mL
2	eggs, at room temperature	2
½ cup	buttermilk	125 mL
⅓ cup	hot brewed coffee	75 mL
2 tsp	vanilla extract	10 mL

1. In a large bowl, using an electric mixer on medium speed, beat applesauce and butter for 1 minute or until well blended. Add cake mix, cinnamon, eggs, buttermilk, coffee and vanilla; beat on medium speed for 2 minutes.

2. If desired, place paper liners in wells. Fill each well with about 1½ tbsp (22 mL) batter. Bake for 6 to 8 minutes or until a tester inserted in the center of a cupcake comes out clean. Transfer cupcakes to a wire rack to cool. Repeat with the remaining batter.

Red Velvet Cupcakes

**Makes
22 to 24 cupcakes**

Pretty enough for a
party, yet easy enough
for every day. Frost
these cupcakes with
Cream Cheese Frosting
(page 90) for a classic
look and flavor.

Tips

Gluten-free all-purpose
baking mix is a blend of
several kinds of gluten-free
flours and starches. The
exact blend used varies
from brand to brand, so
you might prefer the baking
qualities and flavor of one
over another. One popular
brand is Bob's Red Mill, but
stores and websites that
specialize in gluten-free
baking ingredients offer a
large array of brands and
package sizes.

Always read labels to be sure
all products are gluten-free
and were not processed in
a plant that also produces
products that contain gluten.

• Paper liners (optional)

1¼ cups	gluten-free all-purpose baking mix (see tip, at left)	300 mL
3 tbsp	unsweetened cocoa powder	45 mL
½ tsp	baking soda	2 mL
¼ tsp	salt	1 mL
¾ cup	granulated sugar	175 mL
½ cup	butter, softened	125 mL
2	eggs, at room temperature	2
1 tbsp	red food coloring	15 mL
1 tsp	vanilla extract	5 mL
¾ cup	buttermilk	175 mL

1. In a small bowl, whisk together baking mix, cocoa, baking soda and salt. Set aside.

2. In a large bowl, using an electric mixer on medium-high speed, beat sugar and butter for 1 to 2 minutes or until fluffy. Add eggs, one at a time, beating well after each addition. Beat in food coloring and vanilla. Add dry ingredients alternately with buttermilk, making three additions of dry and two of buttermilk and beating on low speed until smooth.

3. If desired, place paper liners in wells. Fill each well with about 1½ tbsp (22 mL) batter. Bake for 6 to 8 minutes or until a tester inserted in the center of a cupcake comes out clean. Transfer cupcakes to a wire rack to cool. Repeat with the remaining batter.

Banana Cupcakes

A light dusting
of gluten-free
confectioners' (icing)
sugar is all the frosting
you need on these tasty
cupcakes. Of course,
if you really want to
gild the lily, they would
be delectable with
Cream Cheese Frosting
(page 90).

Tips

Gluten-free all-purpose
baking mix is a blend of
several kinds of gluten-free
flours and starches. The
exact blend used varies
from brand to brand, so
you might prefer the baking
qualities and flavor of one
over another. One popular
brand is Bob's Red Mill, but
stores and websites that
specialize in gluten-free
baking ingredients offer a
large array of brands and
package sizes.

These cupcakes are delicate
when hot. Remove them
carefully from the wells.

Before preparing this
recipe, read the labels
on all of the ingredients
to make sure they do not
contain gluten.

• Paper liners (optional)

½ cup	almond flour	125 mL
¼ cup	gluten-free all-purpose baking mix	60 mL
¼ cup	white rice flour	60 mL
1 tsp	pumpkin pie spice	5 mL
½ tsp	baking soda	2 mL
½ tsp	gluten-free baking powder	2 mL
Pinch	salt	Pinch
1	egg, at room temperature	1
½ cup	granulated sugar	125 mL
¼ cup	packed brown sugar	60 mL
1 cup	mashed ripe bananas (about 2 medium)	250 mL
3 tbsp	vegetable oil	45 mL
1 tsp	vanilla extract	5 mL

1. In a small bowl, whisk together almond flour, baking mix, white rice flour, pumpkin pie spice, baking soda, baking powder and salt. Set aside.

2. In a medium bowl, using an electric mixer on medium speed, beat egg for 1 minute or until fluffy. Add granulated sugar, brown sugar, banana, oil and vanilla; beat on medium-high speed for 1 minute. Add dry ingredients and beat for 1 minute.

3. If desired, place paper liners in wells. Fill each well with about 1½ tbsp (22 mL) batter. Bake for 6 to 8 minutes or until a tester inserted in the center of a cupcake comes out clean. Using a small offset spatula, carefully transfer cupcakes to a wire rack to cool. Repeat with the remaining batter.

Coconut Cupcakes

● ●

**Makes
34 to 36 cupcakes**

These pretty cupcakes
are perfect just as
they are, but you can
also top them with
a candied cherry or
a sweet candy to tie
them into a holiday
or party theme.

. . . .

Tips

If you have a package of
cake mix larger or smaller
than 15 oz (425 g), measure
out 2$\frac{1}{3}$ cups (575 mL).

Before preparing this
recipe, read the labels on all
of the ingredients to make
sure they do not contain
gluten. In particular, check
the confectioners' (icing)
sugar you use to make
the frosting; some brands
contain starch, which should
be avoided.

● Preheat oven to 350°F (180°C)
● Paper liners (optional)

1	package (15 oz/425 g) gluten-free yellow cake mix	1
3	eggs, at room temperature	3
$\frac{2}{3}$ cup	water	150 mL
$\frac{1}{2}$ cup	butter, softened	125 mL
1 tsp	coconut extract	5 mL
	Buttercream Frosting (page 80)	
2 cups	sweetened flaked coconut	500 mL

1. In a large bowl, using an electric mixer on low speed, beat cake mix, eggs, water, butter and coconut extract for 30 seconds or until moistened. Beat on medium speed for 2 minutes.

2. If desired, place paper liners in wells. Fill each well with about 1$\frac{1}{2}$ tbsp (22 mL) batter. Bake for 6 to 8 minutes or until a tester inserted in the center of a cupcake comes out clean. Transfer cupcakes to a wire rack to cool. Repeat with the remaining batter.

3. Meanwhile, spread coconut in a thin, even layer on a baking sheet. Bake in preheated oven for about 5 minutes or until golden. Let cool.

4. Frost cupcakes with Buttercream Frosting and sprinkle with toasted coconut.

Carrot Cupcakes

· ·

**Makes
38 to 42 cupcakes**

Carrots and pineapple combine to make moist cupcakes everyone will love — whether they follow a gluten-free diet or not.

· ·

Tips

If you have a package of cake mix larger or smaller than 15 oz (425 g), measure out 2⅓ cups (575 mL).

If you can't find an 8-oz (227 mL) can of crushed pineapple, buy a larger can and measure 1 cup (250 mL), spooning the same proportion of pineapple and juice you find in the can into the measuring cup.

Toasting pecans intensifies their flavor. Spread chopped pecans in a single layer on a baking sheet. Bake at 350°F (180°C) for 5 to 7 minutes or until lightly browned. Let cool, then measure.

- Paper liners (optional)

1	can (8 oz/227 mL) crushed pineapple, with juice	1
1	package (15 oz/425 g) gluten-free yellow cake mix	1
1 tsp	ground cinnamon	5 mL
½ tsp	ground nutmeg	2 mL
3	eggs, at room temperature	3
½ cup	butter, softened	125 ml
2 tsp	vanilla extract	10 mL
½ cup	finely shredded carrots	125 mL
¼ cup	chopped pecans, toasted (see tip, at left)	60 mL

1. Drain pineapple into a fine-mesh sieve set over a glass measuring cup. Using the back of a spoon, press down lightly on crushed fruit to drain well. Add enough water to the juice to equal ⅔ cup (150 mL).

2. In a large bowl, using an electric mixer on low speed, beat cake mix, cinnamon, nutmeg, eggs, pineapple juice, butter and vanilla for 30 seconds or until moistened. Beat on medium speed for 2 minutes. Gently stir in pineapple, carrots and pecans.

3. If desired, place paper liners in wells. Fill each well with about 1½ tbsp (22 mL) batter. Bake for 6 to 8 minutes or until a tester inserted in the center of a cupcake comes out clean. Transfer cupcakes to a wire rack to cool. Repeat with the remaining batter.

Pumpkin Cupcakes

● ●

**Makes
38 to 42 cupcakes**

With these cupcakes, you get the convenience of a mix, with all of the rich goodness of Grandma's favorite recipe.

Tips

If you have a package of cake mix larger or smaller than 15 oz (425 g), measure out 2⅓ cups (575 mL).

Before preparing this recipe, read the labels on all of the ingredients to make sure they do not contain gluten.

Be sure to use unsweetened pumpkin purée, not the sweetened, spiced pie filling. If you have a larger can of pumpkin, measure 1¾ cups (425 mL) to use in this recipe and reserve extra for another use.

Toasting nuts intensifies their flavor. Spread chopped nuts in a single layer on a baking sheet. Bake at 350°F (180°C) for 5 to 7 minutes or until lightly browned. Let cool, then measure.

● Paper liners (optional)

1	package (15 oz/425 g) gluten-free yellow cake mix	1
2 tsp	pumpkin pie spice	10 mL
3	eggs, at room temperature	3
1	can (15 oz/425 mL) pumpkin purée (not pie filling)	1
½ cup	butter, softened	125 mL
¼ cup	unsweetened apple juice or apple cider	60 mL
¼ cup	chopped pecans or walnuts, toasted (see tip, at left)	60 mL
¼ cup	mini semisweet chocolate chips (optional)	60 mL

1. In a large bowl, using an electric mixer on low speed, beat cake mix, pumpkin pie spice, eggs, pumpkin, butter and apple juice for 30 seconds or until moistened. Beat on medium speed for 2 minutes. Gently stir in nuts and chocolate chips (if using).

2. If desired, place paper liners in wells. Fill each well with about 1½ tbsp (22 mL) batter. Bake for 6 to 8 minutes or until a tester inserted in the center of a cupcake comes out clean. Transfer cupcakes to a wire rack to cool. Repeat with the remaining batter.

Orange Cheesecakes

Makes 14 to 16 cheesecakes

These cheesecakes deliver a little sweet taste of summer — even when it is cloudy and cold.

Tips

Use a food processor fitted with a metal blade to quickly make fine crumbs from the cookies. You'll need about six 2-inch (5 cm) diameter cookies to make ½ cup (125 mL) crumbs.

If desired, garnish the top of each cheesecake with a drained canned mandarin orange slice instead of the orange marmalade.

Do not let cheesecakes stand at room temperature for more than 2 hours. Always store cheesecakes, sweet or savory, in the refrigerator. When entertaining, set out just those that will be eaten soon, and replenish with chilled cheesecakes as needed.

Variation

Substitute lemon juice and zest for the orange juice and zest. Top with lemon curd instead of orange marmalade.

• Paper liners

Crusts

½ cup	gluten-free shortbread crumbs or sugar cookie crumbs	125 mL
1 tbsp	granulated sugar	15 mL
¼ tsp	ground nutmeg	1 mL
2 tbsp	butter, melted	30 mL

Filling

8 oz	cream cheese, softened	250 g
⅓ cup	granulated sugar	75 mL
1 tbsp	grated orange zest	15 mL
1	egg, at room temperature	1
2 tbsp	freshly squeezed orange juice	30 mL
½ tsp	vanilla extract	2 mL
4 tsp	orange marmalade	20 mL

1. *Crusts:* In a small bowl, combine cookie crumbs, sugar and nutmeg. Stir in butter.

2. Place a paper liner in each well. Spoon about 1½ tsp (7 mL) crumb mixture into the bottom of each liner. Use the pie forming tool to tap crust into liner.

3. *Filling:* In a medium bowl, using an electric mixer on medium speed, beat cream cheese for 1 minute or until fluffy. Beat in sugar and orange zest until smooth. Reduce mixer speed to low and beat in egg until just combined. Beat in orange juice and vanilla just until smooth (do not overbeat).

4. Spoon about 1½ tbsp (22 mL) filling over crust in each liner. Bake for 7 to 9 minutes or until filling is puffed at the edges and softly set at the center. Using a small offset spatula, carefully transfer cheesecakes to a wire rack to cool. Repeat with the remaining crusts and filling. Refrigerate for at least 3 hours, until chilled and set, or for up to 5 days.

5. Just before serving, spoon orange marmalade onto each cheesecake.

Honey Cornbread Muffins

Makes
24 to 28 muffins

Serve these cornbread muffins warm, with butter.

Tips

No buttermilk on hand? Place 2 tbsp (30 mL) lemon juice or white vinegar in a 2-cup (500 mL) liquid measuring cup, then pour in enough milk to make 2 cups (500 mL) total. Let stand for 5 to 10 minutes or until thickened. Proceed with the recipe.

Always read labels to be sure all products are gluten-free and were not processed in a plant that also produces products that contain gluten.

Store leftover muffins in an airtight container and plan to serve within a day or two. Or store in the freezer for up to 3 months.

• Paper liners (optional)

1¾ cups	yellow cornmeal	425 mL
1 tsp	gluten-free baking powder	5 mL
1 tsp	baking soda	5 mL
½ tsp	salt	2 mL
2	eggs, at room temperature	2
1 tbsp	vegetable oil	15 mL
1 tbsp	liquid honey	15 mL
2 cups	buttermilk	500 mL

1. In a large bowl, whisk together cornmeal, baking powder, baking soda and salt. Set aside.

2. In a medium bowl, whisk together eggs, oil and honey. Stir into cornmeal mixture. Stir in buttermilk until just blended.

3. If desired, place paper liners in wells. Fill each well with about 1½ tbsp (22 mL) batter. Bake for 6 to 8 minutes or until a tester inserted in the center of a muffin comes out clean. Transfer muffins to a wire rack to cool slightly. Repeat with the remaining batter. Serve warm.

Brownie Tarts

**Makes
26 to 28 tarts**

No one will ever guess
that these tasty and
pretty brownie tarts
are gluten-free.

Tips

Gluten-free all-purpose
baking mix is a blend of
several kinds of gluten-free
flours and starches. The
exact blend used varies
from brand to brand, so
you might prefer the baking
qualities and flavor of one
over another. One popular
brand is Bob's Red Mill, but
stores and websites that
specialize in gluten-free
baking ingredients offer a
large array of brands and
package sizes.

To melt chocolate chips,
place them in a small
microwave-safe glass
bowl. Microwave on High
for 1 minute. Stir and
microwave on High in
30-second intervals, stirring
after each, until melted.

Serve immediately or store
in an airtight container in
the refrigerator for up to
1 day.

- Paper liners

Tarts

¾ cup	gluten-free all-purpose baking mix	175 mL
1 tsp	instant espresso powder	5 mL
½ tsp	baking powder	2 mL
¼ tsp	salt	1 mL
⅔ cup	butter, cut into chunks	150 mL
3 oz	unsweetened chocolate, chopped	90 g
3 oz	semisweet chocolate, chopped	90 g
1¼ cups	granulated sugar	300 mL
1 tsp	vanilla extract	5 mL
3	eggs, at room temperature	3

Topping

½ cup	granulated sugar	125 mL
8 oz	cream cheese, softened	250 g
1 tsp	vanilla extract	5 mL
13 to 14	small strawberries, halved	13 to 14
¾ cup	semisweet chocolate chips, melted (see tip, at left)	175 mL

1. *Tarts:* In a small bowl, whisk together baking mix, espresso powder, baking powder and salt.

2. In a large heatproof bowl set over a saucepan, over simmering water, melt butter, unsweetened chocolate and semisweet chocolate; stir until smooth. Remove from heat and whisk in sugar and vanilla. Whisk in eggs, one a time, until blended. Whisk until batter is smooth and glossy. Whisk in dry ingredients just until blended.

3. Place paper liners in wells. Fill each well with a heaping tbsp (15 mL) batter. Bake for 8 to 9 minutes or until tarts are softly set (do not overbake). Using a small offset spatula, carefully transfer tarts to a wire rack to cool completely. Repeat with the remaining batter.

4. *Topping:* In a medium bowl, using an electric mixer on high speed, beat sugar, cream cheese and vanilla for 1 minute or until fluffy. Spoon or pipe a dollop of cream cheese mixture on top of each brownie tart. Top each with a strawberry half.

5. Drizzle melted chocolate chips lightly over each strawberry-topped tart.

Mashed Potato Cheese Bites

Leftover mashed
potatoes never tasted
so inviting.

Tip
Garnish each potato bite
with 1/2 tsp (2 mL) sour
cream and/or sprinkle with
minced fresh parsley or
more shredded Cheddar
cheese.

1 1/2 cups	prepared mashed potatoes	375 mL
1/2 cup	shredded Cheddar cheese	125 mL
1/2 tsp	salt or garlic salt	2 mL
1/4 tsp	freshly ground black pepper	1 mL
1	egg, at room temperature, lightly beaten	1
2 tbsp	butter, melted	30 mL
	Nonstick baking spray	

1. In a medium bowl, stir together mashed potatoes, cheese, salt, pepper, egg and butter.

2. Spray wells with nonstick baking spray. Fill each well with about 1 1/2 tbsp (22 mL) potato mixture. Bake for 10 minutes or until potato bites are hot in the center and edges are golden brown. Transfer to a serving plate. Repeat with the remaining ingredients. Serve hot.

Part 4

Party Time

Appetizers

Tomato Bruschetta Cups

Here, we give you bruschetta in a new, easy-to-serve shape! Your guests will love the fresh tomatoes and basil nested in warm, garlic-flavored bread cups.

Tip

Prepare the tomato filling a few hours ahead to let the flavors develop. Cover and refrigerate until ready to serve. Prepare the toast cups and fill them just before serving.

Crusts

1	clove garlic, minced	1
2 tbsp	olive oil	30 mL
8	slices sourdough bread	8

Filling

2	plum (Roma) tomatoes, seeded and chopped	2
1	small green onion, chopped	1
2 tbsp	minced fresh basil	30 mL
1 tbsp	minced fresh flat-leaf (Italian) parsley	15 mL
¼ tsp	salt	1 mL
1 tsp	red wine vinegar	5 mL
	Freshly ground black pepper	

1. *Crusts:* In a small bowl, combine garlic and oil. Set aside.

2. Using a rolling pin, roll each slice of bread until it is very thin. Use the large circle of the crust cutting tool to cut a circle from each slice (discard scraps or reserve for another use).

3. Place 1 bread circle on top of each well and gently press into well with the pie forming tool, making a cup. Lightly brush the inside of each cup with garlic mixture.

4. Bake for 5 to 7 minutes or until toast cups are crisp and golden brown. Transfer cups to a wire rack to cool slightly.

5. *Filling:* In a medium bowl, combine tomatoes, green onion, basil, parsley, salt and vinegar. Season to taste with pepper.

6. Spoon filling into toast cups, dividing equally. Serve immediately.

Phyllo Mushroom Morsels

**Makes
12 phyllo cups**

Melted cream cheese, mushrooms, spinach and artichokes make a winning combination for any appetizer.

Tip

Some grocery stores sell fresh, trimmed, ready-to-use vegetables, such as spinach, at the salad bar. You can buy just the amount you need — no waste or extra spinach to use up.

2 tbsp	butter	30 mL
1	shallot, minced	1
1 cup	chopped mushrooms (any variety)	250 mL
1 cup	lightly packed spinach leaves, chopped	250 mL
2 tbsp	chopped well-drained marinated artichoke hearts	30 mL
3 oz	cream cheese, softened and cut into 1/2-inch (1 cm) cubes	90 g
	Salt and freshly ground black pepper	
12	Phyllo Cups (page 117)	12
	Chopped fresh flat-leaf (Italian) parsley	

1. In a medium skillet, melt butter over medium-high heat. Sauté shallot and mushrooms for 5 to 8 minutes or until moisture evaporates from mushrooms and mushrooms are tender.

2. Stir in spinach and artichoke; cook, stirring frequently, for 2 to 3 minutes or until spinach is wilted. Add cream cheese and cook, stirring gently, until cheese is melted. Season to taste with salt and pepper.

3. Spoon mushroom mixture into phyllo cups, dividing equally. Garnish with parsley. Serve immediately.

Parmesan Herb Potato Cakes

**Makes
16 to 20 potato
cakes**

Scrumptious and
addictive, these
bite-size potato
cakes flavored with
Parmesan cheese,
garlic and chives are
the perfect addition to
any buffet — morning,
noon or night.

Tip
You can substitute finely
chopped green onions for
the chives.

3 cups	frozen shredded hash brown potatoes	750 mL
2	cloves garlic, minced	2
¾ cup	freshly grated Parmesan cheese	175 mL
2 tbsp	all-purpose flour	30 mL
2 tbsp	minced fresh chives	30 mL
1 tbsp	minced fresh flat-leaf (Italian) parsley	15 mL
½ tsp	salt	2 mL
¼ tsp	freshly ground black pepper	1 mL
2	eggs, lightly beaten	2
	Nonstick baking spray	
3 tbsp	sour cream	45 mL
	Additional chopped fresh flat-leaf (Italian) parsley or minced chives (optional)	

1. Place hash browns in a colander and rinse under warm water for 30 seconds. Let stand for about 3 minutes or until thawed and well drained.

2. In a large bowl, combine hash browns, garlic, Parmesan, flour, chives, parsley, salt, pepper and eggs.

3. Spray wells with nonstick baking spray. Fill each well with about 1½ tbsp (22 mL) potato mixture. Bake for 10 to 12 minutes or until browned. Transfer potato cakes to a serving platter. Repeat with the remaining potato mixture.

4. Top each potato cake with sour cream and, if desired, garnish with parsley. Serve warm.

Caramelized Onion Fontina Phyllo Cups

**Makes
16 phyllo cups**

Impress your cocktail party guests with these rich appetizers, perfect for a buffet.

Tip
A combination of wild and button mushrooms is preferred in this recipe.

1 tbsp	olive oil	15 mL
2	cloves garlic, minced	2
8 oz	mixed mushrooms (see tip, at left), chopped	250 g
¼ cup	caramelized onions (see box, below), chopped	60 mL
1 tbsp	minced fresh flat-leaf (Italian) parsley	15 mL
¼ tsp	dried thyme	1 mL
	Salt and freshly ground black pepper	
¼ cup	shredded fontina cheese	60 mL
2 to 3 tbsp	crumbled Gorgonzola cheese	30 to 45 mL
16	Phyllo Cups (page 117)	16
16	flat-leaf (Italian) parsley leaves	16

1. In a skillet, heat oil over medium-high heat. Sauté garlic for about 30 seconds or until fragrant. Add mushrooms and cook, stirring occasionally, for 7 to 10 minutes or until moisture evaporates from mushrooms and mushrooms are tender.

2. Stir in caramelized onions, minced parsley, thyme and salt and pepper to taste; cook, stirring frequently, for 1 to 2 minutes or until onions are hot and liquid has evaporated. Remove from heat and stir in fontina and Gorgonzola to taste.

3. Spoon onion mixture into phyllo cups, dividing equally. Garnish each cup with a parsley leaf. Serve immediately.

Caramelized Onions

The easiest way to caramelize onions is to prepare them in a slow cooker. Thinly slice 5 to 6 sweet onions and place in a 4- to 6-quart slow cooker. Drizzle with 2 tbsp (30 mL) olive oil and 2 tbsp (30 mL) melted butter. Cover and cook on High for 6 to 8 hours or until onions are caramelized. Season to taste with salt and freshly ground black pepper. Let cool, then spoon onions into small airtight containers and freeze for up to 6 months. Let thaw overnight in the refrigerator before use.

To make just enough caramelized onions for this recipe, thinly slice 1 sweet onion. In a skillet, heat 2 tbsp (30 mL) butter or olive oil over medium-high heat. Sauté onion for 5 to 6 minutes or until tender. Reduce heat to low and cook, stirring often, for 15 to 20 minutes or until onions are golden brown and very tender. Season to taste with salt and pepper.

Goat Cheese and Honey Tarts

**Makes
8 tarts**

Sweet honey balances tangy goat cheese in these unique tarts with universal appeal. Kathy's daughter Laura serves them often.

Tips

Toasting walnuts intensifies their flavor. To toast walnuts, spread chopped walnuts in a single layer on a baking sheet. Bake at 350°F (180°C) for 5 to 7 minutes or until lightly browned. Let cool, then measure.

Be sure to serve these tarts as soon as you prepare them so the phyllo cups stay crisp. If you want make-ahead convenience, prepare the phyllo cups and toast the walnuts ahead, then assemble the tarts just before serving.

1 cup	crumbled goat cheese	250 mL
8	Phyllo Cups (page 117)	8
4 tsp	olive oil	20 mL
4 tsp	balsamic vinegar	20 mL
4 tsp	liquid honey	20 mL
2 tbsp	chopped walnuts, toasted (see tip, at left)	30 mL
1 tsp	minced fresh thyme or rosemary	5 mL
1/4 tsp	freshly ground black pepper	1 mL

1. Spoon goat cheese into phyllo cups, dividing equally. Drizzle with oil, vinegar and honey. Sprinkle with walnuts, thyme and pepper. Serve immediately.

Rustic Goat Cheese Tapas

**Makes
16 tapas**

Goat cheese melts into a scrumptious filling in these little appetizers — which would also make a great addition to a brunch menu.

Tip

Part of the fun when serving appetizers is the attractive presentation and pretty garnishes. If desired, garnish each of these tapas with a thin strip of roasted red bell pepper and chopped fresh flat-leaf (Italian) parsley.

Variation

Substitute shredded Cheddar or provolone, or another favorite cheese, for the goat cheese.

Crusts

	Favorite Pie Crust (page 114) or store-bought refrigerated pie crust (see tip, page 192)	

Filling

2	eggs	2
2/3 cup	half-and-half (10%) cream	150 mL
1/3 cup	crumbled goat cheese	75 mL
3 tbsp	chopped drained roasted red bell pepper	45 mL
	Salt and freshly ground black pepper	

1. *Crusts:* Use the large circle of the crust cutting tool to cut 16 crusts, rerolling scraps as necessary. Place 8 crusts evenly on top of wells and gently press into wells with the pie forming tool. Cover the remaining crusts and set aside.

2. *Filling:* In a medium bowl, whisk together eggs, cream, cheese and roasted pepper. Season with salt and pepper. Spoon about 4 tsp (20 mL) filling into each crust.

3. Bake for 8 to 10 minutes or until crust is browned and crisp and a tester inserted in the center of a pie comes out clean. Carefully transfer tapas to a wire rack. Let wells cool for about 5 minutes before repeating, with caution, with the remaining crusts and filling. Serve warm.

Crab Rangoon Cups

**Makes
16 wonton cups**

Your guests will never suspect how quick and easy these are to prepare. Don't let on!

Variation

Substitute a 6-oz (170 g) can of shrimp, drained well and chopped, for the crabmeat.

1	can (6 oz/170 g) white crabmeat, drained well	1
1	green onion, finely minced	1
8 oz	cream cheese, softened	250 g
1/4 tsp	garlic powder	1 mL
1 tbsp	Worcestershire sauce	15 mL
16	Wonton Cups (page 120)	16
1	green onion (green part only), chopped	1

1. In a medium microwave-safe glass bowl, combine crabmeat, minced green onion, cream cheese, garlic powder and Worcestershire sauce. Microwave on High for 1 minute. Stir, then microwave on High in 1-minute intervals, stirring after each, until heated through.

2. Spoon crabmeat mixture into wonton cups, dividing equally. Garnish with chopped green onion. Serve immediately.

Chicken Enchilada con Queso Cups

Makes 18 tortilla cups

Roxanne's friend Lori Vollink shared this recipe with us. Roxanne served it to her brother, who is a hard sell on any recipe, and guess what? He loved it so much that Roxanne's sister-in-law requested the recipe. Thanks, Lori, for sharing.

Tips

If canned chicken is not available, use 1 cup (250 mL) chopped cooked chicken breast, shredded.

Top each baked tortilla cup with a dollop of sour cream or guacamole, if desired.

3	10-inch (20 to 25 cm) flour tortillas	3
1	can (9¾ oz/277 g) chunk chicken breast, drained and shredded (see tip, at left)	1
1	green onion, chopped	1
1	clove garlic, minced	1
4 oz	cream cheese, softened	125 g
¾ cup	shredded Cheddar cheese	175 mL
¼ cup	chopped fresh cilantro	60 mL
½ tsp	chili powder	2 mL
½ tsp	ground cumin	2 mL
½ tsp	ground paprika	2 mL
⅓ cup	salsa	75 mL
18	fresh cilantro leaves	18

1. Working with 1 tortilla at a time, wrap tortilla in a paper towel and microwave on High for about 20 seconds or just until warm. Using the large circle of the crust cutting tool, cut 6 circles from the warm tortilla (discard scraps or reserve for another use).

2. Place 1 tortilla circle on top of each well and very gently press into well with the pie forming tool, making a cup.

3. In a large bowl, combine chicken, green onion, garlic, cream cheese, Cheddar, chopped cilantro, chili powder, cumin, paprika and salsa until well blended. Spoon about 1 tbsp (15 mL) chicken mixture into each tortilla cup.

4. Bake for 7 to 9 minutes or until tortilla cups are crisp and cheeses have melted. Carefully transfer cups to a wire rack to cool slightly. Repeat with the remaining tortilla circles and chicken mixture. Serve warm, garnished with cilantro leaves.

Empanadas with Pork and Caper Filling

**Makes
8 hand pies**

This is one of those special recipes that will lead party guests to stop chewing and ask, "What is in this wonderful filling?"

Tip

If using a store-bought refrigerated pie crust, let come to room temperature, then unroll according to package directions and proceed with the recipe. You can cut 14 Babycakes single crusts from one packaged pie crust (half a 14-oz/400 g package) by rerolling the scraps.

Variations

Substitute ground beef or turkey for the pork.

Stir 1 to 2 tbsp (15 to 30 mL) finely chopped raisins into the filling before spooning it into the crusts.

Filling

2 tsp	vegetable oil	10 mL
4 oz	lean ground pork	125 g
1	clove garlic, minced	1
1/4 cup	chopped onion	60 mL
1/2 tsp	ground cumin	2 mL
Pinch	cayenne pepper	Pinch
1/4 cup	chopped drained roasted red bell pepper	60 mL
2 tbsp	salsa	30 mL
1 tbsp	drained capers	15 mL
	Salt and freshly ground black pepper	

Crusts

	Favorite Pie Crust (page 114) or store-bought refrigerated pie crust (see tip, at left)	
1	egg	1
1 tbsp	water	15 mL

1. *Filling:* In a small skillet, heat oil over medium-high heat. Cook pork, garlic and onion, breaking pork up with the back for a spoon, for 8 to 10 minutes or until pork is no longer pink and onions are tender. Stir in cumin, cayenne, roasted pepper, salsa, capers and salt and pepper to taste; cook, stirring frequently, for 2 minutes or until heated through.

2. *Crusts:* Use the large circle of the crust cutting tool to cut 8 bottom crusts, and use the small circle to cut 8 top crusts, rerolling scraps as necessary. Place large crusts evenly on top of wells and gently press into wells with the pie forming tool.

3. Spoon 1 1/2 tbsp (22 mL) filling into each bottom crust. Place small crusts directly over the center of each filled shell.

4. In a small bowl, whisk together egg and water. Brush lightly over top crusts.

5. Bake for 12 to 15 minutes or until crusts are browned and crisp. Transfer pies to a wire rack to cool slightly. Serve warm.

Fresh Tomato Pizza Bites

**Makes
8 pizza bites**

Pizza is classic party fare, and these little bite-size treats taste a lot fresher than anything you can get from a box.

Variation
For a vegetarian version, omit the prosciutto.

8	Pizza Crusts (page 116), prepared through step 3	8
1	clove garlic, finely minced	1
1/4 cup	shredded mozzarella cheese	60 mL
1/4 tsp	dried oregano	1 mL
3 tbsp	pizza sauce	45 mL
4	grape tomatoes, chopped	4
1/4 cup	finely chopped prosciutto (about 1 slice)	60 mL
2 tbsp	chopped fresh basil	30 mL
4 tsp	freshly grated Parmesan cheese	20 mL

1. Bake pizza crusts for 7 minutes or until crust is set and beginning to dry.

2. Meanwhile, in a small bowl, combine garlic, mozzarella, oregano and pizza sauce. In another small bowl, combine tomatoes, prosciutto and basil.

3. Spoon mozzarella mixture into partially baked pizza crusts, dividing equally. Divide tomato mixture evenly on top.

4. Bake for 5 to 7 minutes or until filling is hot and crusts are crisp. Transfer pizza bites to a wire rack to cool slightly. Sprinkle with Parmesan. Serve warm.

Sausage Balls

• •

**Makes
10 sausage balls**

This recipe was
inspired by an old-time
favorite appetizer from
Roxanne's childhood.
It's quick to prepare,
and it makes just
the right amount for
an appetizer or a
lunchtime nibble.

• •

Tips

To make sure the sausage
balls are fully cooked, test
the center of each ball with
a meat thermometer; it
should read 165°F (77°C).

Cooled baked sausage balls
can be frozen in an airtight
container for up to 1 month.
Reheat from frozen on a
rimmed baking sheet in a
350°F (180°C) oven for 15 to
20 minutes or until heated
through.

4 oz	sausage (bulk or removed from casings)	125 g
¾ cup	baking mix, such as Bisquick	175 mL
½ cup	shredded Cheddar cheese	125 mL
2 tbsp	water	30 mL

1. In a medium bowl, using your fingers, combine
sausage, baking mix, cheese and water, working dough
until well blended. Form into ten 1½- to 2-inch (4 to
5 cm) balls. Place 1 ball in each well (do not use
paper liners).

2. Bake for 4 minutes. Using a small offset spatula,
carefully turn balls over and bake for 4 to 5 minutes or
until dough is browned and sausage is no longer pink
(see tip, at left). Carefully wipe out wells and repeat
with the remaining ingredients.

Dazzling Treats for Holidays and Special Events

Champagne Cupcakes

**Makes
36 to 38 cupcakes**

You don't have to wait for a special occasion to pop the cork. Serve these bite-size celebrations anytime! We like to keep the smaller bottles of champagne on hand to use when preparing these.

Tip

If you prefer, you can substitute a mix of Champagne flavoring and water for the Champagne. Use water and flavoring according to label instructions to equal the 1 cup (250 mL) Champagne. Champagne flavoring can be purchased at bakery supply and kitchen stores.

• Paper liners (optional)

1½ cups	all-purpose flour	375 mL
¾ tsp	baking powder	3 mL
½ tsp	baking soda	2 mL
¼ tsp	salt	1 mL
⅓ cup	shortening	75 mL
1⅓ cups	granulated sugar	325 mL
1 tsp	vanilla extract	5 mL
4	drops red food coloring	4
3	egg whites, at room temperature	3
1 cup	Champagne or sparkling wine	250 mL
	Champagne Frosting (page 87)	

1. In a medium bowl, whisk together flour, baking powder, baking soda and salt. Set aside.

2. In a large bowl, using an electric mixer on medium speed, cream shortening. Beat in sugar, vanilla and food coloring until well blended. Add egg whites, one at a time, beating well after each addition. Add flour mixture alternately with Champagne, making three additions of flour and two of Champagne and beating on low speed until smooth.

3. If desired, place paper liners in wells. Fill each well with about 1½ tbsp (22 mL) batter. Bake for 6 to 8 minutes or until a tester inserted in the center of a cupcake comes out clean. Transfer cupcakes to a wire rack to cool. Repeat with the remaining batter.

4. Frost cupcakes with Champagne Frosting.

Valentine's Day Conversation Heart Cupcakes

**Makes
20 cupcakes**

You will have fun decorating these pink cupcakes for your Valentine. The glaze dries to a semi-firm, glossy coating that is the perfect backdrop for the conversation hearts.

Tips

It's important to use store-bought prepared frosting for this recipe. Cover and refrigerate the remaining frosting for up to 30 days.

Glaze cupcakes immediately after preparing the glaze so that it flows to cover the tops. If it cools, reheat the glaze in the microwave for about 15 seconds on High; stir well.

Use both larger and smaller conversation heart candies to top the glaze.

1/2	container (16 oz/450 g) creamy vanilla frosting	1/2
1/2 cup	white baking chips	125 mL
3 to 4	drops red food coloring	3 to 4
20	Princess Pink Party Cupcakes (page 37)	20
	Conversation heart candies	

1. In a small microwave-safe glass bowl, microwave frosting on High for 45 seconds. Stir in baking chips. Microwave on High for 45 seconds. Stir well. Microwave on High for 15 seconds. Stir until chips are completely melted. Stir in food coloring.

2. Spoon about 1 tsp (5 mL) warm glaze onto each cupcake and spread to coat the tops evenly. Immediately decorate with conversation heart candies.

Alternative Decorations

Omit the conversation heart candies and pipe on your own thoughts instead. Prepare Decorator Frosting (page 89), tinted to the desired shade, and pipe words onto the cupcakes.

Frost the cupcakes with Decorator Frosting (page 89) instead of glazing.

Divide the glaze into batches and color each batch to match the colors of the conversation heart candies.

Select your favorite candies to decorate the cupcakes.

Use a rolling pin to roll out sheets of colored fondant on a cutting board lightly dusted with confectioners' (icing) sugar or cornstarch. Use cookie cutters to cut out heart shapes, then place them on the glaze before it dries.

Easter Basket Cupcakes

**Makes
16 cupcakes**

Springtime means
Easter, and these
little cupcakes make
darling baskets.

Tips

Be sure to use paper liners
when baking the cupcakes,
as they will help create the
look of Easter baskets.

These cupcakes can
be assembled up to
1 day ahead. Store in an
airtight container at room
temperature.

Variations

You can use any flavor of
cupcake for these delightful
baskets. Cupcakes that are
white, yellow, orange or
pink look the prettiest. Tint
the frosting to complement
the cupcakes.

Frost the cupcakes with
Decorator Frosting
(page 89) instead of
Buttercream Frosting.

• Icing bag fitted with a star tip

16	Lemon Cupcakes (page 27), made using paper liners Lemon Buttercream Frosting (page 80)	16
3 tbsp	sweetened flaked coconut	45 mL
2	drops green food coloring	2
16	4-inch (10 cm) pieces red shoestring licorice	16
48	jelly beans	48

1. Lightly frost the top of each cupcake with Lemon Buttercream Frosting, using a knife to smooth the frosting so that it is flat. Fill the icing bag with the remaining frosting and pipe it around the outer top edge of each cupcake so that it resembles a basket.

2. Place coconut and food coloring in a sealable food storage bag. Seal and shake until coconut is evenly colored. Spoon about $\frac{1}{2}$ tsp (2 mL) coconut onto the center of each cupcake.

3. Use a piece of licorice to shape a basket handle for each cupcake, pushing the ends of the licorice down between the cake and the paper liner on opposite sides. Use frosting as needed to help glue handle in place. Place 3 jelly beans in the center of each cupcake, on top of the coconut.

Alternative Decorations

Instead of shoestring licorice, choose twisted licorice. Leave 2 pieces stuck together, so that the basket handle is a little larger and more pronounced. Loosely twist the double strand of licorice so that the handle has a more decorative shape.

To make spring baskets, omit the jelly beans and place tiny sugar flowers (available at cake decorating stores) on each cupcake. Or, for an elegant twist, top each cupcake with miniature edible flower blossoms.

Summertime Cookie and Fruit Cups

Makes 8 cookie cups

No one needs to know how little time these elegant sweets took to prepare. As the cookie dough bakes and then cools, it becomes slightly cupped — the perfect shape for the blueberry filling!

Tips

Wrap leftover dough tightly in plastic wrap and refrigerate for up to 1 day or freeze for up to 9 months. Let dough partially thaw in the refrigerator, then slice and proceed with the recipe or use as desired in another recipe.

Paper liners are a must in this recipe, to protect your fingers from burning.

Select small, fresh blueberries for these cups. Reserve larger berries for a snack or other recipes.

• Paper liners

5½ oz	refrigerated sugar cookie dough (about ⅓ of a 16½-oz/468 g roll)	156 g
⅓ cup	small blueberries (see tip, at left)	75 mL
1 tbsp	granulated sugar (or to taste)	15 mL
⅓ cup	heavy or whipping (35%) cream	75 mL
2 tsp	confectioners' (icing) sugar	10 mL

1. Slice cookie dough into 4 equal slices, about ½ inch (1 cm) wide. Cut each slice in half and shape into a rounded, flat disk about 1½ inches (4 cm) in diameter.

2. Place paper liners in wells. Place 1 dough disk in each well.

3. Bake for 11 to 13 minutes or until cookies are golden brown and edges are crisp. (Cookies will be soft and will harden as they cool.) Using a small offset spatula, carefully transfer cookies to a wire rack to cool completely.

4. In a small bowl, gently mash a few of the blueberries to release a bit of juice; stir in granulated sugar. Let stand for 5 to 10 minutes or until sugar is dissolved.

5. In another bowl, using an electric mixer on high speed, beat cream until frothy. Beat in confectioners' sugar until stiff peaks form.

6. Spoon blueberry mixture into cookie cups, dividing equally. Dollop with sweetened whipped cream. Serve immediately.

Team Favorite Tailgater Cupcakes

Makes
36 to 40 cupcakes

Tailgate time means great food, beverages and fun — no matter which teams are playing. These cupcakes add to the fun, since they can be decorated with team initials or logos. And the addition of dark beer to the batter complements the drink most often consumed at these events!

Tips

Other kinds of beer may be substituted for the dark beer.

Molasses comes from boiling the juice that is extracted from processing sugar cane or beets into sugar. Light (fancy) and dark (cooking) molasses can be used interchangeably in this recipe, but dark molasses will give a more robust flavor.

- Paper liners (optional)
- Tiny alphabet cookie cutters

½ cup	dark beer	125 mL
½ cup	unsulfured dark (cooking) molasses	125 mL
½ cup	vegetable oil	125 mL
¼ tsp	baking soda	1 mL
½ cup	packed brown sugar	125 mL
¼ cup	granulated sugar	60 mL
1⅓ cups	all-purpose flour	325 mL
2 tsp	unsweetened cocoa powder	10 mL
2 tsp	pumpkin pie spice	10 mL
1¼ tsp	baking powder	6 mL
¼ tsp	salt	1 mL
2	eggs, at room temperature	2
½ cup	chopped pecans, toasted (see tip, at right)	125 mL
	Cream Cheese Frosting (page 90)	
	Confectioners' (icing) sugar or cornstarch	
	Fondant	

1. In a large microwave-safe glass bowl, combine beer, molasses and oil. Microwave on High for 1 minute or until boiling. Stir in baking soda and let foam. Stir in brown sugar and granulated sugar. Let cool for 5 minutes.

2. In a small bowl, whisk together flour, cocoa, pumpkin pie spice, baking powder and salt. Set aside.

3. Whisk eggs into beer mixture. Stir in flour mixture and pecans.

4. If desired, place paper liners in wells. Fill each well with about 1½ tbsp (22 mL) batter. Bake for 6 to 8 minutes or until a tester inserted in the center of a cupcake comes out clean. Transfer cupcakes to a wire rack to cool. Repeat with the remaining batter.

5. Frost cupcakes with Cream Cheese Frosting.

200 Dazzling Treats for Holidays and Special Events

Tip

Toasting pecans intensifies their flavor. Spread chopped pecans in a single layer on a baking sheet. Bake at 350°F (180°C) for 5 to 7 minutes or until lightly browned. Let cool, then measure.

6. On a cutting board lightly dusted with confectioners' sugar, roll out fondant to about $\frac{1}{8}$-inch (3 mm) thickness. Using the cookie cutters, cut out the initials of your favorite team. Using the tip of a sharp knife, cut out a team logo or football shapes. Arrange fondant decorations on cupcakes.

Additional Decorations

Cut out triangles from paper in your team colors and tape onto toothpicks for pennants; insert into cupcakes.

Use food-safe edible colored markers to draw laces on the fondant footballs.

Halloween Spooktaculars

Makes
24 cupcakes

Prepare a variety of spooky creatures to add to the fun at your Halloween party.

Tip

Filling an icing bag is easy. Fold the top of the bag down around itself, like a sleeve cuff, so that 2 to 3 inches (5 to 7.5 cm) is folded over. If you are using a decorating tip, push it through the bag to the tip, or add the coupler so that you can change tips while the bag is still full. Spoon the frosting into the bag, filling it about half full. Roll up the sides and twist the top shut. Use a rubber band to prevent frosting from squirting out the top — especially if kids are helping. Then gently squeeze the icing bag from the top down, pushing the frosting out through the tip.

Ghosts

24	large marshmallows	24
24	Chocolate Cupcakes (page 22)	24
	Decorator Frosting (page 89), made with colorless vanilla extract	
72	mini candy-coated chocolate candies	72

1. Glue 1 marshmallow to the top of each cupcake with a small dollop of frosting. Starting at the top of the marshmallow, pipe strips of frosting in parallel lines down to the top edge of the paper liner. Fill in the strips of frosting until the marshmallow is completely covered to resemble a ghost.

2. Use 2 candies to make eyes and 1 candy to make a scary open mouth on each ghost.

Frankensteins or Monsters

24	large marshmallows	24
	Decorator Frosting (page 89), half tinted light green, half white	
24	Chocolate Cupcakes (page 22)	24
	Mini semisweet chocolate chips	
48	½-inch (1 cm) pieces red shoestring licorice	48
	Food-safe edible colored markers	
	Red decorating gel or dark red Decorator Frosting (page 89)	

1. Lightly frost the top of each marshmallow with light green frosting. Dip frosting lightly in chocolate chips so that the chips become hair.

2. Stick a piece of shoestring licorice into the lower side of the marshmallow to become a neck bolt; repeat with a second piece of licorice so that the bolts are evenly spaced on either side of the marshmallow. (If necessary, use the tip of a sharp knife to cut small slits in the marshmallow so that the licorice slides easily into the marshmallow.)

3. Use edible markers to draw faces on marshmallows.

Tips

Let cupcakes cool before frosting — for at least 30 minutes, if possible. If they're frosted while warm, the frosting will melt.

These cupcakes can be assembled up to 1 day ahead. Store in an airtight container at room temperature.

4. Spoon or pipe a dollop of white frosting on top of each cupcake.

5. Use the red decorating gel to make a "bloody neck" on the bottom of each marshmallow, then stick a marshmallow on top of each cupcake.

Big Black Spiders

24	Chocolate Cupcakes (page 22)	24
	Decorator Frosting (page 89), three-quarters tinted black, one-quarter white	
192	3- to 3½-inch (7.5 to 8.5 cm) pieces black shoestring licorice	192
48	mini chocolate chips or tiny candy-coated chocolate chips or candies	48

1. Frost cupcakes with black frosting.

2. Stick 8 pieces of licorice into the top edge of each cupcake, just above the paper liner, to look like spider legs, spacing 4 on one side and 4 on the other. Arch the legs down to the serving platter.

3. Make bulging eyes with a dollop of white frosting and mini chocolate chips.

Martians

• Icing bag fitted with a star tip

	Decorator Frosting (page 89), tinted green	
24	Chocolate Cupcakes (page 22)	24
96 to 120	1- to 1¼-inch (2.5 to 3 cm) pieces red shoestring licorice	96 to 120
72	mini candy-coated chocolate candies	72

1. Fill the icing bag with frosting and frost cupcakes with a peaked swirl.

2. Push 4 or 5 pieces of licorice, standing straight up, into the top edge of the frosted cupcakes to resemble antennae and hair. Make eyes and a nose using candies.

Christmas Chocolate Cranberry Cupcakes

On Christmas Eve, Roxanne's family always indulges in chocolate cranberry cake. These morsels, while inspired by that tradition, are not as rich as the original and are much easier to prepare!

Variation

If desired, add ¼ tsp (1 mL) almond extract to the frosting with the milk.

- Preheat oven to 350°F (180°C)
- Rimmed baking sheet

28 to 30	Chocolate Buttermilk Cupcakes (page 23) Creamy Chocolate Frosting (page 82)	28 to 30
3 cups	cranberries	750 mL
⅓ cup	granulated sugar	75 mL

1. Follow the instructions for Chocolate Buttermilk Cupcakes, but fill the wells with a scant 2 tbsp (30 mL) batter. (You will want more cake to counter the tartness of the cranberries.)

2. Frost cupcakes with Creamy Chocolate Frosting.

3. Spread cranberries in a single layer on a baking sheet. Sprinkle with sugar and stir to coat evenly. Bake in preheated oven for 15 minutes, stirring every 5 minutes, until sugar melts and cranberries glisten from the caramelized sugar. Let cool. Spoon 1 to 1½ tsp (5 to 7 mL) cranberries in the center of each cupcake.

Chocolate Candy Cane Cupcakes

Here is a festive way to create fun at your holiday table. The crunch of candy canes and the richness of devil's food cake make a notable combination.

Tips

No buttermilk on hand? Stir 2 tsp (10 mL) lemon juice or white vinegar into 10 tbsp (150 mL) milk. Let stand for 5 to 10 minutes or until thickened. Proceed with the recipe.

If candy canes are not available, substitute 6 hard peppermint candies, crushed.

Variations

Replace the devil's food cake mix with white cake mix.

Instead of the crushed candy canes, sprinkle each frosted cupcake with coarse red sugar.

• Paper liners (optional)

2 cups	devil's food cake mix	500 mL
2	eggs, at room temperature	2
10 tbsp	buttermilk (see tip, at left)	150 mL
1/4 cup	vegetable oil	60 mL
1/2 tsp	peppermint extract	2 mL
	Peppermint Cream Cheese Frosting (variation, page 90)	
3	medium candy canes, coarsely crushed	3

1. In a large bowl, using an electric mixer on low speed, beat cake mix, eggs, buttermilk, oil and peppermint extract for 30 seconds or until moistened. Beat on medium speed for 2 minutes.

2. If desired, place paper liners in wells. Fill each well with about 1 1/2 tbsp (22 mL) batter. Bake for 6 to 8 minutes or until a tester inserted in the center of a cupcake comes out clean. Transfer cupcakes to a wire rack. Repeat with the remaining batter.

3. Frost cupcakes with Peppermint Cream Cheese Frosting. Sprinkle evenly with crushed candy canes.

White Chocolate Snowmen Cupcakes

**Makes
32 cupcakes**

No need to wait until it snows to make these cold-weather guys. Shaved white chocolate gives them the look of freshly fallen snow, and their charming fondant features will warm your heart! Plus, the cupcakes are so good, you'll be tempted to make them all year long.

Tip

Did you forget to set out the butter so that it will soften? Cut it into slices, place on a microwave-safe glass plate and microwave on Medium-Low (20%) for 10 to 15 seconds or until starting to soften. Let butter stand for about 10 minutes, then proceed with the recipe.

• Paper liners (optional)

Cupcakes

1¼ cups	all-purpose flour	300 mL
1¼ tsp	baking powder	6 mL
¼ tsp	salt	1 mL
¾ cup	granulated sugar	175 mL
6 tbsp	butter, softened	90 mL
2	eggs, at room temperature	2
4 oz	white chocolate, melted (see tip, at right)	125 g
⅔ cup	milk	150 mL

Decoration

	White Chocolate Cream Cheese Frosting (page 91)	
1	3½- or 4-oz (105 or 125 g) white chocolate bar	1
32	gumdrops, cut in half crosswise	32
32	1½-inch (4 cm) pieces red shoestring licorice	32
96	mini candy-coated chocolate candies	96
	Confectioners' (icing) sugar or cornstarch	
	Fondant	

1. *Cupcakes:* In a medium bowl, whisk together flour, baking powder and salt. Set aside.

2. In a large bowl, using an electric mixer on medium-high speed, beat sugar and butter for 1 to 2 minutes or until fluffy. Add eggs, one at a time, beating well after each addition. Beat in white chocolate. Add flour mixture alternately with milk, making three additions of flour and two of milk and beating on low speed until smooth.

3. If desired, place paper liners in wells. Fill each well with about 1½ tbsp (22 mL) batter. Bake for 6 to 8 minutes or until a tester inserted in the center of a cupcake comes out clean. Transfer cupcakes to a wire rack to cool. Repeat with the remaining batter.

Tips

To melt white chocolate, place in a small microwave-safe glass bowl and microwave on High for 30 seconds. Stir and microwave on High in 30-second intervals, stirring after each, until melted.

Be sure to buy standard, or medium-size, gumdrops for the earmuffs, not the jumbo ones.

4. *Decoration:* Frost cupcakes with White Chocolate Cream Cheese Frosting.

5. Using a vegetable peeler, scrape down the side edge of the white chocolate bar to make shavings. Sprinkle shavings over frosting, giving it a "freshly fallen snow" look.

6. Place 2 gumdrop halves, cut side down, on opposite sides of each cupcake to make earmuffs. Arrange 1 strip of red licorice to look like a mouth and use candies to make eyes and a nose.

7. To make hats, on a cutting board lightly dusted with confectioners' sugar, roll out fondant to about $\frac{1}{8}$-inch (3 mm) thickness. For the center of each hat, cut a piece of fondant about 2 by $\frac{3}{4}$ inches (5 by 2 cm). Fold it in half so it becomes a rectangle of about 1 by $\frac{3}{4}$ inch (2.5 by 2 cm) (the double thickness will hold the shape of the hat better and be stronger). For the hat band, cut a strip of fondant about 3 by $\frac{1}{2}$ inches (7.5 by 1 cm). Place the hat band over the edge of the rectangle, folding the ends under so that the hat band is the right size for the hat. Position a hat on the top edge of each cupcake.

Caramel Pecan Chocolate Candy Cups

**Makes
16 candy cups**

These elegant treats come together incredibly quickly — perfect for the busy holiday season. They are very rich, so this is one time where you could allow one per guest.

Tips

Dulce de leche is similar to caramel topping and can usually be found in the grocer's baking aisle or the Latin foods aisle, or at a Latin market. Use leftover dulce de leche as a topping for ice cream.

If you use a whole toasted pecan on each candy cup in place of the chopped pecan pieces, this treat will resemble a traditional Turtle-type candy.

²/₃ cup	dulce de leche (see tip, at left)	150 mL
16	Phyllo Cups (page 117)	16
½ cup	semisweet chocolate chips	125 mL
¼ cup	chopped pecans, toasted (see tip, page 201)	60 mL

1. Spoon a heaping teaspoon (5 mL) of dulce de leche into each phyllo cup.

2. Place chocolate chips in a small microwave-safe glass bowl. Microwave on High for 30 seconds. Stir, then microwave on High for 20 to 30 seconds or until chocolate is melted and smooth. Dollop chocolate on top of dulce de leche.

3. Sprinkle with pecans. Let stand at room temperature until chocolate is set or freeze for 3 to 5 minutes to speed setting.

Resources

The Electrified Cooks, LLC:
www.electrifiedcooks.com

Kathy and Roxanne's blog, filled with recipes, tips, classes and more: www.pluggedintocooking.com

Select Brands: www.selectbrands.com

Babycakes: www.thebabycakesshop.com

Cake Decorating Supplies

Beryl's: www.beryls.com

Fancy Flours: www.fancyflours.com

N.Y. Cake: www.nycake.com

Sweet! Baking & Candy Making Supply: www.sweetbakingsupply.com

Wilton: www.wilton.com

Kitchen Utensils, Kitchen Equipment, Spices, Serving Platters and Packaging

Bridge Kitchenware: www.bridgekitchenware.com

Crate & Barrel: www.crateandbarrel.com

Sur la Table: www.surlatable.com

Williams-Sonoma: www.williamssonoma.com

Flours, Sugars, Spices, Extracts and Premium Ingredients

C&H Pure Cane Sugar: www.chsugar.com

The Stafford County Flour Mills Co.: www.hudsoncream.com

King Arthur Flour: www.kingarthurflour.com

Land O'Lakes: www.landolakes.com

Penzeys Spices: www.penzeys.com

Library and Archives Canada Cataloguing in Publication

Moore, Kathy, 1954-
    175 best babycakes cupcake maker recipes : easy recipes for bite-size cupcakes, cheesecakes, mini pies and more! / Kathy Moore, Roxanne Wyss.

Includes index.
ISBN 978-0-7788-0283-9

    1. Cupcakes. 2. Cake. 3. Pies. I. Wyss, Roxanne II. Title. III. Title: One hundred seventy-five best babycakes cupcake maker recipes.

TX771.M66 2011   641.8'653   C2011-903017-9

Index

Be sure to visit our website

for product reviews, community tips, great recipes, decorating ideas and more!

www.thebabycakesshop.com is your online home for all things Babycakes®. Peruse the full line of Babycakes baking appliances, order accessories and utensils, view photos and recipes from the Babycakes experts and share tips with fellow Babycakes enthusiasts. At www.thebabycakesshop.com, fun and delicious treats are always just a click away!

connect with the Babycakes community online.

discover tips and tricks to make your baking experience even more fun.

create your own recipes and tips and upload photos to share.

www.thebabycakesshop.com

babycakes™
cake pops

Whoopie Pies

Cupcakes & Pies

Classic Donuts